ARIS & PHILLIPS HISPANIC CLASSICS

GABRIELA MISTRAL

Selected Poems

Translated

by

Paul Burns and Salvador Ortiz-Carboneres

with an Introduction by

Paul Burns

Aris & Phillips Hispanic Classics are published by
Oxbow Books, Park End Place, Oxford OX1 1HN

ISBN 0 85668 763 4   978 0 85668 763 1 (cloth)
ISBN 0 85668 764 2   978 0 85668 764 8 (paper)

British Library Cataloguing-in-Publication Data
A catalogue record of this book is available from the British Library

CONTENTS

III. FELLING

IV. WINE PRESS

V. POEM OF CHILE

LIST OF ILLUSTRATIONS

Sources: nos. 1–9, 14, 16: Casa-Museo de Gabriela Mistral, Vicuña, by kind permission of the Director, Sr Rodrigo Irribaren Aviles; 10–13, 15, 17–19: Paul Burns

PREFACE

This is the second collaboration between Salvador Ortiz Carboneres and myself, the first being *Antonio Machado: Lands of Castile and other poems*, published by Aris & Phillips in 2002 (reprinted in 2006). The choice of Gabriela Mistral was his: I did not – to my shame – know her work, but she immediately appealed to me, for the work itself, for the remarkable personality that lay behind it, and also for the fact that she was Chilean. My paternal grandfather, David Burns, went to Chile in the 1870s as representative of the Bank of Scotland and there married Clara Swinburn, descended from a long line of Basques who first emigrated there, as did so many, in the seventeenth century, distinguishing themselves as politicians, merchants, agriculturists, viticulturists, and, later, artists. The first Scottish entry by marriage into a roll call largely of Echazarreta, Errázurriz, and Irigoyen was one Diego Kirk in the 1830s. I had been briefly to Chile in 1987, when I met a welcoming group of second cousins, found the ruins of my grandparents' house, destroyed in the great earthquake of 1906 (after which they moved to London), near the railway station in Viña del Mar, and stood by the Swinburn mausoleum in Santiago's cemetery, realizing that it contained more of my ancestors than any other one place on earth.

With this translation well advanced, my wife and I combined a major birthday of mine in February 2004, celebrated with equal numbers of Chilean relatives and family and friends from England in Viña del Mar, with a pilgrimage to the Elqui Valley, Gabriela Mistral's birthplace. We stayed in a delightful little *residencia* in Vicuña and visited Montegrande and Pisco Elqui (formerly La Unión). As had happened to Antonio Machado in Soria, our 'prophet,' admired by some but condemned by many as a 'deserter' from Chile in her lifetime, was by now very much with honour in her own country. The Casa-Museo dedicated to her in Vicuña, standing with a reconstruction of the house where she was born at the end of a main street named after her, is elegant, evocative, and moving. Its director, Don Rodrigo Irribaren Aviles, was sympathetic to the translation project and most helpful over the supply of most of the illustrations. I also found there the only copy I have seen of the complete *Poema de Chile*, published after Mistral's death, enabling us to include a representative selection from each geographical area as the last part of this book. Montegrande is totally Mistral-centred, and one of the best experiences of the visit was to receive a round of applause from a group of schoolchildren at her tomb when I told them I was translating her. She is – rightly – revered at least as much as a teacher and promoter of children's rights as she is as a writer.

The Spanish texts reproduced here are taken from *Desolación – Ternura – Tala – Lagar* (Ed. Porrúa, Mexico City,1998, introduced by Palma Guillén de Nicolau) and the above-mentioned *Poema de Chile* produced for the Casa-Museo, which bears no publisher or date but has a Prologue by Jaime Quezada, taken from other works dated 1994 and 1995.

Paul Burns   Stowell, December 2005

INTRODUCTION

Chile to the Time of Gabriela Mistral[1]

Around the time of Gabriela Mistral's birth (1889), there was a tendency among Chile's historians, epitomized by the 'General History' of Barros Arana, which set the tone in schools for fifty years, to regard everything that preceded the declaration of independence in 1810 as Spanish, Catholic, and evil. Nevertheless, earlier periods left deep distinguishing marks on Chile's people, and the colonial years from 1535 cannot simply be dismissed as contributing nothing of worth. Equally they cannot be viewed through the later rose-tinted spectacles of *Hispanidad*, worn by apologists who saw the whole conquest of Latin America as a uniquely beneficial exercise in civilization and evangelization.[2]

1. Pre-Conquest

The first human habitation is thought to date from the Ice Age between 25,000 and 40,000 years ago, when waves of migrants from Siberia and Mongolia crossed the ice bridge from Asia to Alaska and gradually made their way down both American land-masses as far as Patagonia. There are no written records until very much later, but elements of the various civilizations that occupied parts of the strip of land cut off from the rest of the continent by the Andes have been pieced together from archaeological remains, aided in the north by the extreme dryness of the Atacama desert region, which has preserved mummified bodies dating from as far back as 5,000 BCE – two thousand years earlier than the Egyptians.

By around 500 BCE there were settled agricultural communities in the north of present-day Chile (the *Norte Grande*) and farther south, in the *Norte Chico* (the region where Gabriela Mistral was born). By 1,000 CE a culture known as the Diaguita emerged in the *Norte Chico*; it was to dominate the region until the Spanish conquest. (Mistral takes a Diaguita boy on her imaginary north-south journey that makes up the context of her last – posthumously published – work, the 'Poem of Chile'.) Other groups had meanwhile settled in areas farther south, and in the fourteenth century these groups coalesced to form the culture known as Mapuche, forming a 'nation' that neither the Incas nor the Spaniards were ever to conquer.[3]

The Incas developed a highly sophisticated civilization in Peru between the twelfth and fifteenth centuries and in 1443 began to expand southward, building an impressive network of roads as they went. The peoples they conquered were forced to pay tribute to the Inca emperor and to speak Quechua. Then in 1532 Spanish *conquistadores* landed on the coast of Peru, finding the Inca empire torn apart by civil war and ripe for conquest by Pizarro's small but well-armed band, aided by the importation of European diseases to which the native population had no immunity.

2. The colonial period

In 1535 Diego de Almagro was charged with extending the conquest southward and followed an Inca road down the spine of the Andes, reaching almost as far south as the site of present-day Santiago. But his expedition failed to find the gold and silver he had been led to expect and returned to Cuzco after appalling sufferings at the hands of the weather and the natives. Three years later Pedro de Valdivia was granted a licence to colonize Chile and set off down the same road with a mere ten compatriots and a group of native bearers. After a year's journey he had reached the river Mapocho, where he founded the city he named Santiago de la Nueva Extremadura – Santiago for St James (the Greater), the patron saint of Spain who had inspired the reconquest of the country from the Moors, completed in 1492 with the fall of the kingdom of Granada, and 'new Extremadura' because the Extremadura region of Spain had long been the south-western border of reconquered territory. Valdivia wrote to the emperor Charles V that, 'This land is such that there is none better in the world to live in.' He has been called the first Chilean, but he should share that honour with the woman he took with him, Doña Inés Suárez, who brought chicken, sheep, and seeds of wheat, all of which she even managed to rescue from an attack when the Indians burned the new settlement. She thereby started the transformation of the landscape and the economy. Within three years of the foundation of Santiago, the first vines had been planted, and it seems that a Spanish olive tree seedling, one of only three survivors from a shipment to Lima, found its way south, so that by the end of the sixteenth century Chile was exporting olive oil to Peru.[4]

Twelve years after the foundation, Valdivia met a horrific death at the hands of the Mapuche, who were brilliantly led by a former stable-boy of his, named Lautaro. He laid waste most of the new settlements and trained his warriors not to expose themselves to Spanish musket fire. Further expansion southward came to a halt, with the Spanish population, which by then had grown to some 5,000, concentrated in the coastal area from La Serena in the north to Concepción in the south. Lautaro was finally killed, and the Mapuche retreated south of the Bío-Bío River, where they held their territory throughout the colonial period.[5]

Chile was by this time being administered on the same lines as the rest of the

Spanish empire, but it remained a remote and unprofitable part of it. The authority of the king of Spain was absolute, and his instructions were handed down by the Council of the Indies. This had a local governor (Valdivia being the first), advised by a high court. The governor had the power to grant land to colonists and equally to 'grant' them the ownership of indigenous people who happened to live on it. This system, known as *encomienda*, was supposed to ensure good treatment of the natives and their conversion to Christianity, but it generally meant their ruthless exploitation in mines and on huge agricultural estates. It began the emergence of the *hacienda* system of ownership of huge estates by often absentee landlords, which was to dominate rural Chile, helped by the *mayorazgo* law by which estates could be passed to the eldest son without being divided. It has lasted largely unchanged, despite attempts at reform in the mid-twentieth century (referred to in 'Poem of Chile') and Salvador Allende's more radical efforts, which led to the military coup and his death in 1973.

Colonists born in Spain called themselves *peninsulares* and remained at the top of the social pyramid; those born in Chile but of Spanish parentage on both sides were *criollos* and saw themselves as hardly inferior, especially as they became relatively more numerous. As the original inhabitants increasingly died out from old-world diseases – though not before Spanish male colonists had interbred with their women – the working classes became increasingly mixed – *mestizo* – and to this day the dominant physical characteristic of the bulk of the population could be described as Eurasian. In the eighteenth century fruit plantations and vineyards flourished, printing was introduced by the Jesuits, and the first two universities were founded.

3. Independence

In 1808 Napoleon Bonaparte invaded Spain and forced King Ferdinand VII to abdicate, replacing him with his brother Joseph (whom the Spaniards unfortunately but appositely nicknamed *Pepe botellas* – Joe bottles). Spanish cities organized local resistance groups, and this pattern was followed in Spanish America, led by the *criollo* section of society. In Santiago a six-man *junta* took control of the city in October 1810, pledging loyalty to the person of the king but implementing several reforms on its own authority. The following November José Miguel Carrera placed himself at the head of a more radical group, which devised a Chilean flag and produced a Constitution that declared valid only laws promulgated within Chile. This effectively changed 'royalists' into 'patriots' and produced an invasion by the Viceroyalty of Peru, supported by the new 'royalist' (mainly *peninsular*) element in Chile. Carrera failed to repel the invasion and was voted out of office and replaced with General Bernardo O'Higgins, 'the Liberator', who held off the royalist forces to greater effect. But in 1814 Carrera seized power once more, the royalist army took advantage of the situation and advanced on Santiago. O'Higgins mounted a last-ditch stand at Rancagua but was overwhelmed. The royalists marched into Santiago, the patriot leaders fled to Mendoza in Argentina, and the first attempt at independence (known as *La Patria Vieja*, 'The Old Country') had collapsed.

Napoleon again influenced the next stage when he was defeated in Spain and Ferdinand VII regained the throne. Ferdinand tried to revert to centralized rule from Spain, convincing an increasing number throughout the continent that they had to seek full independence. In the south the Argentine general José de San Martín was mobilizing an 'army of the Andes', reinforced by Chilean patriots, led by O'Higgins, after the 'disaster of Rancagua'. In February 1817 the army crossed the Andes and O'Higgins defeated the royalists at Chacabuco, to the north of Santiago. The following April San Martín won a conclusive victory at Maipú, and Chilean independence was finally secured. San Martín refused leadership of the new republic, and O'Higgins was elected 'supreme director', exercising a mainly enlightened dictatorship to 1823. He invited Lord Thomas Cochrane to equip a flotilla, which sailed north and landed an expeditionary force under San Martín's command. This captured the port of Callao but failed to occupy the whole of Peru, as had been the original intention. San Martín handed over command to the Venezuelan liberator Simón Bolívar. The failure of the expedition, coupled with the fact that O'Higgins was becoming unpopular for imposing high taxes to pay for the war, forced him to step down in 1823. Despite his attack on Peru (which secured its independence in 1821) he was able to retire there – he was the illegitimate son of a former viceroy – and died there in 1842.

4. *The developing republic*

As elsewhere on the continent, the early decades of independence were marked by struggles between conservative and liberal tendencies, but Chile secured an enduring conservative Constitution and administration earlier than most, mainly due to an outstanding minister (never president), Diego Portales. The Constitution he devised in 1833 aimed at 'order with freedom' and effectively replaced the crown with wide presidential powers, supported by a powerful landowning oligarchy. It did, though, equate the State with the nation and make the rule of law supreme, based on the civic education of the people, according to the British model. It lasted for ninety-two years (so over four decades of Gabriela Mistral's life) and its successor of 1925 was not very different. Portales himself, appointed Minister of War, was assassinated by opponents of his invasion of Peru (which had been annexed by Bolivia) in 1838, an act that increased support for his policy and led to the defeat of the Peru-Bolivia Confederation at the battle of Yungay and the return of Peru and Bolivia to their former separate identities. This was followed by a forty-year period of growth and prosperity, which saw a boom in copper and silver mining, the building of railways, the foundation of the University of Chile, and a growing population, with European immigrants, arriving via a regular steamship route, developing hitherto virtually untouched areas. By the 1850s Chile alone of the Latin American nations felt strong enough to warn of the dangers from the North in the shape of the Monroe Doctrine. This period became known as 'the decades', with four presidents each ruling for a decade. Its ethos was authoritarian and paternalistic, followed by a swing back towards liberalism under President Errázuriz Zañartu from 1871 to 1876. The Araucanians were finally pacified, the arts flourished, and the major cities began to take on the expansive European style they still retain. All this was ended by a world recession that brought Chile's exports to a virtual halt.

In 1878 Bolivia reneged on an agreement not to raise duties on nitrates mined by Chileans in the *Norte Grande* around Antofagasta (ceded to Bolivia) and so sparked the War of the Pacific. Chile invaded Antofagasta in February 1879; Peru, invited to mediate, was bound to Bolivia by secret treaty and so drawn in on Bolivia's side two months later. Both sides saw that security depended on naval supremacy in the Pacific, and the Chilean and Peruvian fleets joined battle. Peru had the advantage in possessing an ironclad, the *Huáscar*, which in May 1879 had the Chilean flagship, the old wooden *Esmeralda*, pinned to the coast off Iquique. The Chilean commander Arturo Prat leapt on board the *Huáscar* when this rammed the *Esmeralda* and died with sword in hand on its deck, making him Chile's greatest national hero. Three months later the *Huáscar* was captured in the battle of Angamos, and Chile went on to secure the area of the nitrate fields and, in January 1881, to capture Lima itself. After two further years of fighting, the Treaty of Ancón gave Chile the former Peruvian province of Tarapacá and what had been the coastal portion of Bolivia, adding a third to its territory and restoring its fortunes with huge nitrate exports free of duty payable to Bolivia but taxed by the Chilean State.[6] The United States tried to impose its own conditions, but Chile stood its ground, stating that it had won the war on its own and was not going to have arbitrary solutions imposed from outside.

This economic boom with accompanying stability lasted until the 1890s, when the increasingly autocratic presidency of José Manuel Balmaceda forced Congress to refuse to approve his budget, leading to civil war. The army supported the president, while the navy supported Congress, which was then able to use nitrate revenues to train its own army, which defeated Balmaceda's forces near Valparaíso. Balmaceda shot himself. The legislature now increased its power through an unstable period up to the First World War. At the same time, industrialization increased rapidly, as did the country's transport network. Conditions for the workers in the all-powerful nitrate industry were appalling,[7] and a labour movement began to develop. When it promoted strikes, these were generally ruthlessly suppressed, the worst episode taking place in Iquique in 1907, when two hundred people, workers and their families, were shot. The World War caused the collapse of the nitrate industry and produced growing civil unrest. Elected in 1920 to carry out bold social reforms, President Arturo Alessandri found himself frustrated by Congress and could achieve relatively little. (One reform he did introduce was the requirement for all teachers in state schools to have received a professional formation: this caused Mistral, who had none, considerable embarrassment.) A military junta – against the tenor of Chilean history but setting a precedent for the events of 1973 – ousted the cabinet in 1924 and made the president appoint senior officers in place of ministers. They were actually more radical and effective, but Alessandri found himself unable to work with them and fled to Argentina. Then a rival junta seized power the following year and invited him back. He redrafted the Constitution, returning power to the president at the expense of Congress, introducing universal suffrage, and separating Church and State. Again, though, he found himself unable to work with the leader of the junta, Carlos Ibáñez, who took over the presidency in 1927. He initially promoted social reform and increased the country's overall standard of living, but, as in 1914, outside events intervened, this time in the shape of the Wall Street crash of 1929. After a period of social unrest and political manoeuvring, Alessandri assumed the presidency once more in 1932.

Four decades of relative calm followed (during most of which Mistral held consular posts outside the country), with presidents from the centre-right Radical Party leading a regeneration of the economy during the 1930s. From 1938 to 1952, three Radical Party presidents oversaw a great expansion of industrialization, which also led to increased inflation and consequent discontent. Carlos Ibáñez returned, as elected president, in 1952, followed by Jorge Alessandri, son of Arturo, in 1958, when a swing to the left almost led to the election of socialist Salvador Allende (the year after Mistral's death). This greatly alarmed the landowners, who threw their weight and influence over the way their workers voted into securing a conservative victory, followed in 1964 by that of the Christian Democrat Eduardo Frei. He, however, was to prove more radical than they expected, embarking on a serious programme of land reform and giving the State a 51% stake in the copper industry. So international capitalism and the United States in particular were already sufficiently alerted not to tolerate Salvador Allende's nationalization of the industry after the narrow victory of his Unidad Popular coalition in the 1970 election, beginning a period that Gabriela Mistral was fortunate not to live to see.

Life of Gabriela Mistral

1. *Childhood and Youth*

She was born Lucila Godoy Alcayaga on 7 April 1889 in Vicuña, a small town in the province of Coquimbo, in the area known as the *Norte Chico* – the little north – some three hundred miles north of Santiago and forty miles inland from the now flourishing resort of La Serena. Vicuña is the gateway to the Elqui Valley, home of the muscatel grape used to make *pisco*, the sweet clear brandy used to put the kick into Chile's national drink, pisco sour, and new vineyards now cling to every possible hillside as well as covering the valley floor. In Gabriela's time the produce was less commercial and more varied, with almond, peach and other fruit trees. The valley features time and again in her poems and in diaries written up to the end of her life: 'There are evenings when I don't know where I am (for all that matters to me . . .). And evenings when memories of the Elqui Valley seize me like those whirls of air do dead leaves.'[8] 'The Elqui Valley is the narrowest slash a traveller could find in any country. You walk up it as though one of your sides is touching one hillside and the other the one opposite, along a corridor of wild mountains' (244).

Figure 1. Gabriela Mistral at the time of her First Communion

Her father, Jerónimo Godoy Villanueva, came from the 'great north' of the arid wastes of the Atacama desert stretching up to the Peruvian frontier, where it never rains. He worked as a schoolteacher in La Unión,[9] the highest village in the Elqui Valley, where he had married, and to which the family moved back when Lucila was a mere ten days old – so the fact that she was born in Vicuña was mere chance. He abandoned the family when she was just four. Her mother, Petronila Alcayaga Rojas, who worked as a dressmaker and seamstress, took her and an elder half-sister (from an earlier marriage of her father's), Emelina, to live in Montegrande, a few kilometres down the valley from La Unión. Lucila was to write, 'En la aldea de La Unión me hicieron. Y en la otra, Montegrande, me crié. Esta es la realidad', 'In the village of La Unión they made me. And in the other, Montegrande, I grew up. This is the truth' (21). In fact Emelina, who was a schoolteacher, effectively took charge of her upbringing.

When Lucila was twelve the family moved to the coast, to the seaside city of La Serena. Her paternal grandmother, Isabel Villanueva Herrera de Godoy, lived there, in a room rented from nuns and in a mental state not quite bordering on insanity, apparently brought on by her two daughters running away to become nuns. She told Lucila to go on loving her father and was responsible for encouraging her to read the Bible (learning 'my father David's' psalms by heart), which had a lasting effect

Figure 2. Emelina with a group of her pupils

on her life and her work. She began to write at the age of eleven, and by the time she was fourteen local papers in La Serena and Vicuña were publishing prose pieces and poems by her. These had a distinctly socialist tinge and were responsible for her being refused entry into the secondary school in La Serena in 1903, even though she had passed the necessary entrance exams. Her diaries of the period are full of adolescent self-preoccupation, with successive aphorisms spelling out how proud, haughty, invulnerable she had to be . . . and never was. She had previously not attended school but been educated by Emelina, a course she was now obliged to continue. She was then given a place in the *Lycée* in La Serena but was expelled for showing 'subversive tendencies' (23). Just after her expulsion, apparently, she walked down to the beach, obviously depressed. The Provincial Governor happened to see her and asked what was making her so sad. She told him, and he appointed her teacher in a village just outside La Serena, La Compañía Baja. She was only fifteen at the time, and at least one of her pupils, a boy, was a year older. From there she was posted to La Cantera, where she taught children in the daytime and workers in the evening. She did this for two years, until she was eighteen. Together with her time in Montegrande, she wrote, teaching in La Cantera 'made my soul'.[10]

2. First love, recognition, teaching

Tall and slim, with fair hair and green eyes, she met and fell seriously in love with a young railway worker, Romelio Ureta Carvajal. 'Amo, amo, amo. Es decir, tengo hecha miel la sangre, hechos música los suspiros,' she wrote: 'I love, I love, I love. That is to say, my blood is turned to honey, my sighs to music' (40). He was not as serious with her and had other women friends. They broke off the relationship, and he took up with a girl from a family 'with pretensions to grandeur', with whom he could not keep pace financially. He stole money from the railway company and was on the point of marrying her when, on 25 November 1909, he shot himself. A postcard from Lucila was found in his pocket and although it was two years since

8

Figure 3. G.M. aged seventeen

they had been *novios*, she was deeply upset by the incident. She had written several love poems inspired by him, and his suicide prompted many of the poems that were later to make her famous, starting with 'The Sonnets of Death', though she did not try to publish these till many years later.

Lucila lived and taught in small towns or villages, but she had friends in the capital, where she used to go to use the public libraries (even if she found Santiago pretentious and bombastic, and lacking the pre-conquest history of Mexico City and Lima). Her friends encouraged her to take the supplementary exams required for a licence to teach in secondary schools. She passed these with distinction, and after a year spent in Triague she was appointed history teacher in Antofagasta, in the *Norte Grande*. After a year there she was moved to Los Andes, some fifty miles north of Santiago, where she stayed from 1912 to 1918, by which time she was twenty-nine. (She was probably not aware of the fact, but Chile's only canonized saint, Teresa of Los Andes, was then growing up in the same town, preparing to enter the Carmelite convent, which she did the year after Lucila left, only to die of typhus the following year. She was canonized in 1997 and is often referred to as America's 'little saint' on account of her similarity to the 'little flower', St Thérèse of Lisieux.) Lucila lived on the outskirts of the town and taught geography and Spanish in the secondary school for girls. The Head of the school, Doña Fidelia Valdés Pereira, whom Lucila referred to as a 'chosen soul', encouraged her writing, and her six years in Los Andes were both peaceful and productive. She had time to read and did so widely: Rabindranath Tagore, Maurice Maeterlinck, Amado Nervo, Romain Rolland, Shakespeare (whom she called 'the man for all centuries'), and others.

She continued writing poetry, prose poems, and prose pieces. Theosophy – fashionable at the time – became a major influence, along with Eastern philosophy. She taught herself the technical aspects of versification from manuals and from her reading of other poets. In Los Andes she met Pedro Aguirre Cerda, a future President (1938–41), then Minister of Justice and Education, who, with his wife, helped and supported her; he was the only politician to whom she ever felt she owed any gratitude. She began using the pseudonym Gabriela Mistral, and this name (made up either of the Archangel Gabriel or the Christian name of Gabriele D'Annunzio plus the surname of Frédéric Mistral) became generally accepted as hers, not just as a *nom de plume* (and so is now used here). She first came to general notice as a poet when 'The Sonnets of Death', written in the wake of her *novio*'s suicide, were published in 1914 and won first prize in the Floral Games organized by the Chilean Society of Writers and Artists. Famous from then on, she was accepted as a colleague by the leading Chilean writers of the time. She wrote contemptuously of the competition, calling it the 'most odious thing in the world . . . Games, Prizes, fame. Nothing!' (48), but it led to an enduring friendship at least bordering on love with one of the jurors, the poet Manuel Magallanes Moure, with whom she carried on a correspondence lasting six years.[11] She felt herself maturing, relying less on intuition than on observation, and learning to accept people as she saw them. She complained of the lack of respect accorded to women writers in Chile – brought about, as she saw it, by the way men pretended to notice their works while really caring for nothing but their eyes. . . . (53). She described her six years in Los Andes as 'the most intense of my life', not just because she had written nearly all her poems there, but because she had been able to concentrate on the real purpose of her life: teaching. Literature, she wrote, had never been 'an end for me. . . . My sensitivity, what little culture I have, my great enthusiasms, I have all given to teaching' (62).

She moved to the southern end of the country in 1918, when, on the recommendation of Pedro Aguirre Cerda, she was appointed Head of a secondary school in Punta Arenas, on the Magellan Straits, the most southerly city in Chile. Her task was twofold, to reconcile warring factions in a school 'divided against itself', and to help in the 'Chilenization' of a region in which foreign influences were then dominant. She spent two years there, during which she wrote some of the best poems later published in her first collection. She opened a night school in which workers – who were mostly illiterate – could study without paying fees. In 1920 (after refusing another recommendation by Pedro Aguirre Cerda to a post in La Serena)[12] she was nominated to another Headship, in Temuco, the largest city in southern Chile and gateway to the Lake District, where Pablo Neruda was born and went to school. There she came to know and appreciate the Araucano Indians – and to castigate Ercilla's epic as boring, false, dead. She remarked on the 'greatest fatigue that can be seen in this world' on the faces of the men and on the gentle, poetic language of their womenfolk.[13] A year later she left 'that city of bitter memory for me' when Aguirre Cerda, now Minister of Public Education, appointed her Head of the new 'No. 6 School for Girls' in Santiago. She still disliked Santiago and had wanted to move to Argentina, but her mentor, Aguirre, would not hear of her leaving the country. This, though, was the period in which the government insisted on professional qualifications for all teachers. Mistral railed against 'bad men' in her diaries, declaring that her qualifications came not from a piece of paper but from her heart and from God: 'God put me here. He is with me in my bitterness and strengthens me in righteous protest' (80). Nobody had bothered when she was earning a pittance reorganizing schools in the provinces, but now that she was in the capital, even her professional association turned against her. That year, 1921, she received news that Federico de Onís, then Professor of Spanish at Columbia University, had given a lecture on her poetry, which led to an initiative by staff and students at the 'Institute of the Spains' in New York to issue a collection of her published and unpublished verses. This volume appeared as *Desolación* in New York in 1922.

3. Overseas

She then received an invitation from the rector of Mexico University, José Vasconcelos,[14] to join a team working on an educational reform programme for the whole country. As a teacher, Gabriela was a government employee, and the Chilean government not only gave her permission to go but added a commission to study the proposed reforms and see what could be adopted with advantage in Chile. She spent some two years in Mexico, helping to organize rural literacy campaigns and mobile libraries. She also edited a splendid anthology of 'Readings for Women', including many pieces of her own writing, which was published by the Public Education Secretariat in Mexico. She rejoiced in the light, the climate, and the mountains, similar to those of her native Elqui Valley. She admired the Indians for their intuitive art, was amazed at the respect given to artists, but exhausted by the

11

Figure 4. G.M. in Mexico, 1923/4

number of invitations to lecture. She hated the intellectuals for their cliques and superficiality, excepting only Vasconcelos as her one true friend and supporter, who stood head and shoulders above all others. She supported him passionately in his mission to educate the Indians, returning to being a rural teacher. She travelled all over the country by train and on horseback, sleeping in Indian villages and grand colonial mansions, savouring the endless variety of the cooking and the unfailing courtesy of the people. Mexico was for her the best of the Spanish-American 'race'; she saw it in the relatively early and tolerant years of 'revolutionary' government under President Alvaro Obregón, leaving just two years before the 'Calles law' of 1926 unleashed the Cristero uprising and years of virtual civil war, undoing many of her hopes for the future of the country.[15]

In 1924 her friend and correspondent Manuel Magallanes Moure died. It was four years since they had corresponded, and she was able to write of him dispassionately. Her diaries contain a panegyric of which anyone might be proud (108–11). Towards the end of the same year she travelled to Europe for the first time, visiting Spain, France, Italy, Belgium, and Switzerland. She interviewed literary figures in these countries, and these interviews, as well as other essays, appeared in prestigious newspapers and reviews in both Europe and America. On her return to Chile, which she felt she was seeing objectively for the first time – and hated for the greed of the middle classes, the lack of agrarian reform, the absence of ideals – in 1925, she retired from teaching, to which she had devoted twenty years, being rewarded with a modest pension (thanks to the strange appointment to the rank of 'State teacher', notified to her by telegram in Mexico, to which she did not even deign to reply). She was appointed adviser to the Ibero-American Letters section of the League of Nations Institute for Intellectual Cooperation – the forerunner of UNESCO. The post was based in Paris, and she sailed to France via Buenos Aires, where she enjoyed evenings of tango in the cabarets. In Paris she worked on producing English and French versions of Latin American classics, while representing Chile in two other institutes: as these were all honorary posts, she had to supplement her very meagre teacher's pension with journalism. Even that pension was lost when she attacked the military *junta* that had taken over the government of Chile, which suspended it in reprisal.[16] She wrote more for the newspapers and carried on. Paris (including nearby Fontainebleau where she lived) was cold and expensive: she longed for sunnier climes and a cheaper life. Saddened by events in Mexico, especially the 'stupid and senseless' closing of Catholic schools, and in Nicaragua, where the United States intervened militarily against Sandino, she wrote passionately on both (113; 261–2). She felt she had lost her reason for living when her mother died in La Serena in 1929: 'My mother's death has destroyed me, reduced me really to ashes. Not even my faith sustains me; I just raise my eyes a little' (111; see 117, 120–1). It also left her with the expense of maintaining the house in La Serena as well her own. She moved first to Provence, then to a series of villages on the Ligurian coast, where she could live very cheaply, dreaming of proceeding even farther south, to Naples, Algiers, Tunis. . . . Her work left her time for artistic and intellectual contacts: among others, she met and was impressed by two influential figures of the time, Giovanni Papini, author of *The Life of Christ* (1921, Eng. trans. 1923), and Romain Rolland, author of the ten-volume novel *Jean-Christophe* (1902–14), which Gabriela admired as a passionate plea for social justice.

Invitations to lecture in the USA began in 1930. She moved to Puerto Rico for three years, dividing her time between lecturing in America and her work for the Institute in Europe. In 1932 the Ibáñez regime in Chile was replaced by a civilian government under the presidency of Arturo Alessandri Palma (of whom she, initially at least, had a low opinion), and her pension was restored. She was appointed honorary consul in Naples, where her beloved nephew Juan Manuel Godoy was

Figure 5. G.M. arriving on her visit to Chile in 1938

attending an Italian school. Mussolini's Fascist regime refused to confirm her appointment, nominally 'on economic grounds' but in her view because 'the fine medieval regime does not accept women in such posts. . . .' The following year she was moved to Madrid, still with no salary – just with the prestige of officially representing her country. She hated Castile, hated the endless stream of petitioners at the consulate, felt more of a foreigner in Spain (excepting Catalonia) than anywhere else. The consular office paid less than half her expenses and she was rapidly exhausting the personal savings she had managed to accumulate in the United States and Puerto Rico. Pablo Neruda was living in Madrid but with a post as assistant consul in Barcelona and longing to be appointed consul in Madrid, and she tried to arrange an exchange with him, as a gesture of help to him and because she much preferred Barcelona. She appealed to Pedro Aguirre Cerda for a substantial loan, and in mid-1935 a group of distinguished writers, including Miguel de Unamuno, Georges Duhamel, Romain Rolland, and Ernst Curtius appealed to President Alessandri, asking that she be given a paid consulship in keeping with her reputation. In September the Chilean Senate responded by appointing her 'life consul', with a salary that enabled her to live either in Europe or in America. There were no conditions attached, but she felt duty-bound to set up a proper consul's office wherever she lived and to carry out normal consular tasks. News of this in the Chilean press, exaggerating her appointment to 'Consul General', produced a wave of protest against someone who had become a 'foreigner', who had only two years consular service and was, furthermore, a woman and an ageing one at that (135–6).

The following month, October 1935, she was appointed not to Barcelona but to Lisbon (while Neruda did get the appointment to Madrid). She lived in Portugal till

1937 – thereby escaping the horrors of the Spanish Civil War. From Lisbon she travelled to Paris to oversee the publication of volumes in the Latin American classics series. In 1937–8 she lectured widely in South America, and her second collection, *Tala*, was published. It contained poems written over the previous fifteen years, some of the best recently in Portugal. It had a more mixed reception than 'Desolation', with one critic complaining that he could not understand even the title – which usually means 'tree felling', but in Chile can mean 'grazing' and in Puerto Rico 'vegetable garden'. Her Argentine publisher, Victoria Ocampo, gave all the proceeds to help Spanish children forced out of their homes by German and Italian bombing in the Spanish Civil War. Gabriela included a rapid visit to Chile in her tour, in May 1938. She travelled south from Santiago by train, admiring the countryside she had not seen for many years and noting the expansion of agriculture. She visited the cities of Concepción and Chillán: seven moths later the latter was totally destroyed and the former very badly damaged in an earthquake that affected a third of the entire country.

From Portugal she welcomed the election of her friend and supporter Pedro Aguirre Cerda as president of Chile on 24 December 1938 – a welcome tempered by his threat, in a letter to her, to bring her back to Chile 'by force', in the only fascistic action of his presidency, and by rumours that Ibáñez (the 'eternal sergeant', as she called him) and his supporters were planning a military coup. In 1939 a group of writers in Ecuador began a campaign for her to be awarded the Nobel Prize for Literature. This gradually broadened and gathered momentum, but the process required funds and hard work, and she had at least one other well-placed Latin American rival. She herself was more concerned with events in Spain and trying to organize the evacuation of Spanish professors to America. At the same time she worried about political developments in Chile, where ideas rooted in Italian and German fascism seemed to be gaining ground. She defined her stance as 'non-internationalist socialist . . . in the sense of wanting our future to be *criollo* Americanist' (149–50).

On the outbreak of World War II in September Gabriela was in Nice, but shortly afterwards she was posted to Brazil, first to Niteroi, where the humid climate did not agree with her, then to Petrópolis, in the mountains above Río and Niteroi, where she felt better. More supporters joined in the campaign for her to be awarded the Nobel Prize (suspended during the war). She continued to take a keen interest in the Chilean political situation, writing a Prologue to the future (1964) Christian Democrat president Eduardo Frei's political manifesto, *La política y el espíritu* (1940). In 1941 President Aguirre Cerda died suddenly, causing her great shock and distress.

Her nephew (whom she called Yin-Yin), who had lived with her since 1928, had accompanied her to Brazil and lived with her. He was a source of great joy to her, but this joy turned to sorrow when, in August 1943, at the age of just seventeen, he apparently killed himself by swallowing arsenic in the wake of some student quarrel

Figure 6. G.M.'s nephew, Juan Manuel Godoy, 'Yin-Yin'

involving pro-Allied (his) and pro-Nazi factions, which, magnified by adolescent fervour, became a matter of life and death for him. Gabriela was at his bedside when he died. The shock seems to have had a lasting effect on her health, and she was treated for what Brazilian doctors took for 'tropical amoebas' (later diagnosed in the U.S. as diabetes). She struggled between her Catholic faith and Eastern influences, which suggested to her that his death was her *karma* and had to be punishment for some crime she had committed in an earlier incarnation. He appeared to her one night, and she convinced herself this was to tell her that Jesus Christ had forgiven him and that he had reached heaven and was at peace. Her emotions over his death were expressed in a series of poems in her next collection, *Lagar* (Wine Press), not published till 1954, eleven years after the event.

4. The Nobel Prize and after

After the end of World War II in 1945 the Chilean Writers' Association and the government renewed her candidature for the Nobel Prize for Literature, and the first post-war prize was awarded to her. The government ordered her to collect it in

Figure 7. G.M. receiving the Nobel Prize for Literature from King Haakon of Norway, 1945

Stockholm in person, which she did after a terrible Atlantic crossing in December 1945. She found that the award changed her life: 'People give me things I never deserved and never even dreamed of' (175). She received invitations to England, France, and Italy, in all of which her work was beginning to be known in translation and admired. All over the American continent(s) she found herself the focus for what she called 'an American militia of a spiritual order'. She never returned to Brazil and used the prize money to buy a house in California, near Los Angeles, from where she moved to Santa Barbara in 1948.

By now her health was deteriorating, though U.S. doctors treated her diabetes and her advancing loss of sight, which they restored in one eye. She also felt very much alone, especially after the death in July 1947 of her half-sister Emelina, who had effectively brought her up, with no 'bond to sect, party, or even clan' (178), though she did have a few good friends in whom to confide. She also found it hard to write as a Nobel Prize winner, not helped by a considerable volume of hate mail from Chile, calling her Communist, deserter of her country, lazy writer, even lesbian. . . (178). What hurt perhaps most was the accusation of being rich: on the lowest rank of consular salary, she earned $426 a month, and her necessary expenses were more than double that. The difference had to be made up by renting out half her house and from her writing. In an interview with President Truman she told him that the 'yankee' view of the inhabitants of the southern part of American continent was distorted and that what they needed was not so much investment as being heard, understood, and granted free visas.

In November 1948 she accepted an official invitation from President Alvaro Obregón to return to Mexico, conveyed by the Minister of Education, the poet Jaime Torres Bodet. As she stepped down from the plane in Yucatán, she collapsed, and she was unconscious for three hours. She was revived and spent two months as a guest of the government, after which she stayed on privately. Mexico City was considered too high for her health, and she settled in the State of Veracruz, where she received a steady stream of literary and other visitors from the capital. The government proposed to give her a plot of land there on which to build a house, but a muddle over the site meant that the deal fell through, and she returned to the USA in December 1949.

After lecturing in Washington, DC, she sailed to Europe once more, settling on the Italian coast, first at Rapallo and then in Naples, where she was appointed consul. Delighted to be back in her 'sweet Europe' (apparently forgetting her earlier opinion of Castile), she nevertheless suffered terribly from the winter cold – one kidney had been damaged by the climate in Punta Arenas years earlier, and her circulation was very bad. Her diary entries from these years oscillate between alarm at the situation in Chile (where President González Videla was undertaking land reform but her *bête-noire* Ibáñez was gathering wide support and was to be returned to power in 1952), memories of her childhood in the Elqui Valley, and reflections on her formative reading, significant episodes in her life, her health, and advancing old age. She was offered the post of head of UNICEF in America but refused this, becoming a counsellor for UNESCO instead. Chile awarded her its National Prize for Literature in 1951, but she was too ill to collect it in person and donated the prize money to the children of the Elqui Valley.

Early in 1953 she was appointed Chilean consul in New York and sailed from Genoa to make her home in Roslyn Harbor on Long Island. Before settling there, she went to Cuba, accepting an invitation to attend the centenary celebrations for José Martí. Then, having made some sort of peace with President Carlos Ibáñez ('the repentant enemy of today'; 229), she made a final journey to her homeland in August and September 1954, sailing to Valparaíso on board the SS *Santa María*. In Santiago she was greeted by enthusiastic crowds, whom she addressed from the

Figure 8. G.M. in Montegrande, 1954

balcony of the presidential palace, La Moneda. She was given prizes and a Doctorate *Honoris Causa* by the University of Chile. In the Elqui Valley she was received like the queen she had said, many years before, she was going to be: 'But in the Elqui Valley, with its / hundred mountains or more, / the others who came are singing, / and those who come will sing: / "On earth we shall be queens / and we shall reign for real, / and as our kingdoms are so vast, / we shall all reach the sea"' ('We were all going to be queens', published in *Tala*, 1938; see pp. 96–101). She also travelled south, to re-visit schools and people, and to observe plants for inclusion in her 'Poem of Chile'. While she was there the fourth edition of *Desolación* was published in Santiago, followed in December by *Lagar*, containing poems written between 1938 and 1954.

There were further honours to come: she was awarded a Doctorate *Honoris Causa* on her return to USA by the University of Columbia, in a ceremony shared with Konrad Adenauer, Dag Hammarskjöld, and Adlai Stevenson. The final section of her diaries, titled 'of farewells' and covering 1955 and 1956, contains memories of flowers of the Elqui Valley, of things her mother taught her, together with brief thoughts on her age and failing health: the last entry reads; '*Se me va todo, se nos va todo. Apenas puedo despedirme.*' 'I am losing everything, we are losing everything. I can scarcely say farewell' (237). In 1955 she nevertheless managed to attend the celebrations for the seventh anniversary of the Universal Declaration of Human Rights at the U.N. General Assembly in New York, where, in her final public act, she read a message: 'I should be happy if your noble effort to obtain Human Rights were to be adopted faithfully by all the nations of the world. This triumph would be the greatest of those achieved in our time' (290). Her health declined sharply during 1955 and 1956. Doctors misdiagnosed the causes for some months, but after a violent haemorrhage she was found to have cancer of the pancreas. After a spell in hospital in New York, she was moved to Hempstead General Hospital on Long Island, where she died on 10 January 1957. The United Nations General Assembly paid formal tribute to her on the day of her death. Her funeral service was held in St Patrick's Cathedral on 14 January, following which her body was flown back to Chile. There was a further funeral service in Santiago General Cemetery on 23 January, after which her body remained in a vault there till 1960, when, as she had requested, it was finally laid to rest in a special tomb in Montegrande. This is now a national monument. Set on a hillock just above the village, it looks out over the valley with its vines. The tomb itself is approached by steps rising through clumps of local plants, and her beloved schoolchildren go there in busloads.

Gabriela Mistral's Work

The volume of Gabriela Mistral's published work, taking all her articles for the press into account, is quite substantial; within that, poetry forms a relatively modest portion, but it was certainly the part that meant most to her. In a diary entry from 1946, written in California, she refers to hostile Chilean reactions to the award of the Nobel Prize, which included 'being lazy and a writer of books'. Quantity, she wrote, was never a preoccupation: 'I do not have the taste for an abundance of [books], nor the vanity to produce book after book. I write like someone constantly beginning to learn the language, and I attach no transcendence to what I do' (178). Her poetry, however, stemmed from a basic impulse:

Figure 9. G.M.'s funeral service in Vicuña church, 1960

I write poetry because I cannot disobey the impulse, it would be like blocking a spring surging up in my throat. For so long now I have been the servant of the song that arrives, that presents itself and that cannot be buried. How can I seal myself now? . . . I know intuitively what I do: I do not possess that knowledge other writers have, able to expound their features or their devices like giving a lecture on mineralogy. Each poem is an adventure down fresh paths, even with unknown weapons and animals. . . . I start with a feeling that gradually puts itself into words, helped by a rhythm that might be that of my own heart [which had an irregular beat]. . . . I used to be a scandalous romantic. *Desolation* barely floats on so much syrup. I learned, later, from the classics and from life, not to burn so showily, like the Pamplona Fair, so as to burn better, with a long glow, with a hidden brand, like the Greeks of all ages. . . . I look for primordial words, which name outright, words that will not rust or wear, hard as the hawthorn axles of my Montegrande carts. (224–5)

Many of her poems were published in papers and periodicals some years before being collected into volumes. She certainly did not produce 'book after book': collections published during her lifetime were basically three, later rearranged into four volumes.[17] These are:

1. *Desolación* (Desolation). First published in 1922 by the Institute of the Spains, New York. It contained sections of poems for children, later extracted and published separately as

2. *Ternura* (Tenderness). Published by Editorial Calleja, Madrid, 1924. Second edition, revised and augmented by other poems for children originally published as four sections in *Tala*, published by Editorial Losada, Buenos Aires, 1945;

3. *Tala* (Felling). First edition by Editorial Sur, Buenos Aires, 1938, collecting poems written since the publication of *Desolación* sixteen years earlier. Second edition by Losada, 1947, without the poems for children removed to *Ternura*;

4. *Lagar* (Winepress). Published by Editorial Pacífico, Santiago, 1954, collecting the work of a further sixteen years, since the publication of *Tala*.

She had been working intermittently on a long, open-ended poem about Chile at the time of her death. Originally to be titled *Recado de Chile* (*recado*, meaning 'message', being a favourite form of communication of hers, generally in prose). This was eventually published as *Poema de Chile* by Editorial Pomaire, Barcelona, in 1967. Her prose works would fill at least four substantial volumes. Selections of both verse and prose have been published regularly since the award of the Nobel Prize to her, including seven selections of prose writings between 1957 and 1995.[18]

She is essentially a lyric poet, dealing with the eternal themes of lyric poetry: love, loss, happiness, sorrow, death, nature. They are all subjects of various sections in all her published volumes of poetry. Her individuality lies in her approach to the great themes: she has a certain savage honesty, using words that echo the emotions – primordial words, as she said. This, as well as her themes, remains constant throughout her work, though her tone overall progresses from an emphasis on sorrow to greater serenity. Each of her volumes represents the work of a good number of years, and within each she deliberately constructed thematic sections that do not correspond to when each poem was written, so there is little point in attempting to discern her biography from her work. Some events she does indeed refer to, such as the suicide of Romelio Ureta and, much later, the death of her mother, but it does not follow from this that all poems following 'The Sonnets of Death' dealing with death and sorrow in 'Desolation', for example, also refer to him. (The book's title in fact refers to the landscape of Patagonia and is that of the first poem in the 'Nature' section, not to her feelings after the death of Romelio.) She loved other men, but these loves may not be reflected only in poems that appear later in the book: she was constructing a poetic work, not an account of herself in verse.

Influences that remain constant, though in shifting terms, are her faith and her love of nature. In later life she called herself a 'total Catholic', but it is by no means certain that this would be seen by others as true at the time, and she certainly embraced non-orthodox beliefs, such as reincarnation, at times in her life. Nature, equally, shifts from being an earthly paradise to which to return in another life on earth, or the glory of God shown in a foretaste of a permanent Christian heaven. She read widely in Oriental traditions, but she also progressed in knowledge of Christianity way beyond the conventionally pious Catholic upbringing in the Hispanic mould she would have received. She has been called a mystic poet, and she certainly knew and admired St Teresa of Avila and St John of the Cross, but she makes no attempt to describe the essence of divinity or union with God, as they do. She frequently displays a love of nature verging on pantheism – or, more accurately, panentheism, a sense of God's indwelling in nature rather than nature being God, in the Franciscan mould.

One aspect that sets her apart from most other lyric poets is her professional – and passionately held – concern with education. She was an idealist with feet firmly on the ground, in that she rooted her ideals in twenty years experience as a 'rural schoolteacher'. Her ideal education had nothing to do with modern concepts of utilitarianism; it aimed at encouraging children to become conscious of their value as individuals, in themselves and in their relationships with others, with the animal kingdom, with the whole of creation, and with God. Songs were an integral part in this formation: hence her continuous production of verse for children.

'Desolation', in its final form, after the removal of the children's verses that were moved to 'Tenderness', contains sixty-four poems, arranged in four sections: 'Life', 'School', Sorrow', 'Nature'. 'School' has only two poems (and might more logically have been removed with the children's verses); the two longer sections. 'Life' and 'Sorrow' are not particularly homogenous in tone.[19] The latter, as has been noted, cannot be read as a coherent account of a tragedy and the poet's reaction to it, despite earlier critical attempts to do so. The object of her despairing love is secondary to her feelings of love, and love itself is sorrowful. The order of the poems within the section probably deliberately suggests one love for a man (Romelio Ureta)) when there were two, the second being Manuel Magallanes Moure.[20] Mistral herself contributed to the autobiographical quest in the 'Vow' attached to the end of the book, in which she says, 'In these . . . poems lies bleeding a painful past in which song became bloodied to relieve me.' But the 'vow' was that she would 'climb to spiritual plateaux where a broad light will fall on my days. From there I will sing the words of hope. . . .' The poems themselves have been considered a mixture of 'perfect' and 'irregular and rough' (Arce): the dichotomy – if it really exists – is certainly not a reflection of any lack of skill on Mistral's part. She is mistress of the precise word needed, and much of her subject matter is 'rough'. Their style has been compared to that of the parables of the New Testament, the earthiness of which would certainly have appealed to her in her quest for a poetry that reflected the very earth of her origins and with which she identified. This identification gives rise to the mother's love for a son that fuses with a woman's love for a man, as seen in the 'Sonnets of Death' and other poems of sorrow. Much has been made of the sorrow of Gabriela's physical childlessness and resultant feeling of incompleteness as a woman, but this is often subsumed in her identification with 'mother earth' – which she interestingly refers to using (well before it became fashionable) the Greek term *Gaia*, rather than the Amerindian *Pachamama*, as might have been expected. 'Earth', she wrote, 'adopts the posture of a mother with a child in her arms (with her creatures in her wide arms)'.[21] It is also subsumed in her embracing of teaching as an evangelical mission and her passionate concern for all the children of the world.

'Tenderness' contains over a hundred poems, arranged in seven sections. Mistral herself added a final note, 'Colophon by way of excuse', which provides the best description of her conception of lullaby as verse for mothers and children – 'as being something the mother presents to herself and not to the child who can understand nothing.'[22] Noting that lullabies are an oasis in the desert of women's paucity of musical composition, she calls them 'a day- and night-time colloquy of a mother with her soul, with her child, and with the Gaia visible by day and audible by night.'[23] In America, she notes, women of Spanish descent are probably still singing adaptations of lullabies that came over 'with the caravels', but there is a need for a native tradition because the names of plants and other familiar objects are so different. So these are an attempt to provide a basis for one, even if a tradition cannot be forced. . . . The poems here, she knows, are far from her ideal of folklore; they are an invitation to musicians to get them moving – an invitation that has in fact been taken up in Chile, Mexico, and Argentina. Even if they proved of no use to anyone, she would continue writing them, because in her own hard life she has always welcomed sleep as a gift from God, and lullabies eventually send the mother to sleep as well as the child.

Songs to accompany children's games, 'Rondas', are another category. Latin Americans again have to invent, with no medieval tradition on which to draw: born 'monstruously' out of the sudden clash between native populations and European colonizers, they cannot call on 'seven centuries of Middle Ages', as the Italian, Provençal, and Spanish cultures can. And yet it is vital for *criollo* children to have their own songs, games, and dances, and if there are no words for them, then poets such as she have to go on trying to produce new songs, even if the 'Holy Spirit does not come down' and no blessed Child-Messiah has yet brought 'the grace of the children's genre'. The test of her verses is to hear children reciting them, and if they make changes or mistakes, this is because the poems are still not quite right, and so she goes on making changes, ever searching for a perfect children's language.

As 'Tenderness' collects children's verses from the period covering the composition of 'Desolation' as well as the succeeding sixteen years, so 'Felling' in its usual form has a similar genesis, in that the original (1938) edition also included lullabies and other children's verse, which were later removed.[24] Its publication was brought about by her desire to help the child refugees of the Spanish Civil War, to whom she gave the royalties earned.[25] Referring to her part-Basque ancestry (the inheritance of so many Chileans), she laments the ungenerous response of Latin America to the refugee crisis of Basque children, forced instead into less friendly climes and cultures and to wrestle with unknown languages. The title, considered obscure at the time, refers to the cutting-back process in her own life through various losses and probably also in the life of the world through war, and the book begins with a section titled 'Death of my Mother'. The poems selected here all have an element of loss or deprivation: of native country, of childhood, of dreams, of objects lost or never possessed. Yet the book is not a lament: the 'felling', or paring down, is a necessary preparation for writing and a form of liberation. It has been seen as a landmark book in not only Chilean but all South American poetry, containing the roots of all that is Indo-American (Jaime Quezada).

'Wine Press', first published in 1954, continues many of the same themes, with the additional stratum of powerful poems reflecting the horrors of the Second World War (see pp. 116–9; 120–3; 126–7).[26] The process of paring down her own *persona* is dramatically illustrated by 'The Other', in which she states baldly that she killed one side of herself because the other (the literary figure of Gabriela Mistral) had driven out the original (Lucila Godoy). It is a book of nostalgia and of melancholy, but also of final liberation from all ties extraneous to her work. In 'The Last Tree', which on its own forms an Epilogue to the book, she relinquishes both sides of herself, 'the loneliness I gave myself' and 'the loneliness they gave me'. Her 'pass[ing] through the world in dream, race, or flight' both sums up all the alienations to which she felt subjected and at the same time hints at the basic concept of the 'Poem of Chile', in which she journeys as a ghost.

This ghost is accompanied on a voyage from north to south of the country by a Diaguita (from the *norte chico* area in which she grew up) Indian boy and a *huemul*,[27] thus combining her maternal instinct with her love of Indian-ness and the natural beauties of Chile. The 'Poem of Chile', published posthumously in 1967, makes no mention of the nation's historical or political history; the author's identification is with the flora and fauna and landscape. It shows no trace of nationalism, of an ideal of Chile as a community of inhabitants: Mistral is relating to an ecological entity, not a human one, for which her feeling is maternal, not fraternal.[28] She is affirming her close relationship, despite years of living elsewhere, with the deepest roots of the country: pre-Columbian cultures and their surviving traces, mountains, rivers, animals, fruits, herbs, and, crops.

The poems were written over a long period, as shown by earlier publication of individual poems in other collections, but probably organized into the final project towards the end of her life. She wrote that children were the best judges of language, and this project, with its ubiquitous diminutives, its dialogues and its colloquialisms, seems to be addressed to them. It is a worthy final offering to those she loved as a universal, spiritual mother and to the land she loved also with a frustrated maternal love, feeling it always with her wherever she went but also knowing how much of it escaped her in her absence.[29]

Notes

1. The main source for this section is the straightforward and objective 'A Brief History of Chile' in Melissa Graham, *The Rough Guide to Chile* (2d ed., 2003), pp. 549–69. Other sources consulted include 'Chile: Four Centuries of History' in *Chile Today* (n.d. but after the Pinochet coup of 1973), pp. 2–12; Jaime Eyzaguirre, *Fisonomía Histórica de Chile* (Mexico City, 1948; 15th ed., Santiago, 1999).

2. This tendency is evident in, *inter alia*, Eyzaguirre (n. 1, above).

3. They eventually recognized the sovereignty of the king of Spain over the rest of the country but never over their territory. Their 300-year war against the Spanish produced deeds of great heroism on both sides and relatively early in its course inspired the poet Alonso de Ercilla to write his epic *La Araucana* (described by Mistral as dying within fifty years from the literary death 'of mortal boredom'). See Dana Gardner Munro, *The Latin American Republics* (London: Harrap, 1961), p. 44.

4. See Germán Arciniegas, *Latin America: A Cultural History* (London: Barrie and Rockliff, The Cresset Press, 1967).

5. Partly because the War of the Pacific followed relatively soon on the American Civil War (1861–5), it went largely unnoticed in the Anglo-Saxon world. Those – especially boys – with Chilean antecedents, nurtured on Harry Collingwood's *Under the Chilean Flag*, had at least a one-sided view of it.

6. As reflected in the work of various writers of the period, such as Baldomero Lillo (1867–1923), whose short stories include 'El Chiflón del Diablo', in F. Sepúlveda and M. Pereira, eds., *Cuentos Chilenos* (Santiago, 4th ed., 2001), pp. 149–64.

7. Cited in *Bendita mi lengua sea: diario íntimo de Gabriela Mistral (1905–1956)*, edited by Jaime Quezada (Santiago, 2002), p. 236. Individual entries are not dated, but this is in the final section, from 1956. This work is a principal source for this section, and future page references are given after quotations in the text. The other principal source is the 'Datos biográficos' provided by her friend Palma Guillén de Nicolau, in Gabriela Mistral, *Desolación – Ternura – Tala – Lagar* (Mexico City: Ed. Porrúa, 1973, 8th ed., 1998).

8. In 1939 the local councillor (and future president of Chile), Gabriel González Videla, re-named La Unión 'Pisco Elqui', in a blatantly commercial move designed to prevent Peru claiming exclusive rights to the name *Pisco* (a town in Peru where the brandy was originally made).

9. She later related the circumstances in a letter to Pedro Aguirre Cerda. *Bendita*, pp. 70–73.

10. Her letters to him are collected in *Cartas de amor de Gabriela Mistral* (Santiago, 1978). He is often regarded as the second great love reflected in the pages of 'Desolation'.

11. Her letter to him is dated 1 Feb. 1920.

12. American Indians and 'Indian-ness' became one of the great themes of her writing and

the injustices done to them a central preoccupation of her life. For her comments on the Araucano Indians see *Bendita*, pp. 72–5.

13. José Vasconcelos (1882–1959), writer, philosopher, educator. Appointed rector of University of Mexico in 1920. Editor of the review *El Maestro*. On 8 July 1921 instituted the Secretariat for Public education and Fine Arts, which had previously been devolved to individual States. 'Teacher and tyrant,' he wrote, 'are two mutually exclusive terms. By contrast, teacher and freedom are synonymous; that is why free peoples venerate their teachers and are concerned to improve their schools.'

14. On the *Cristero* uprising and subsequent strife see E. Dussel (ed.), *The Church in Latin America; 1492–1992* (Tunbridge Wells and Maryknoll, NY, 1992), pp. 223–4.

15. For governments in Chile during this period, see editor's notes in *Bendita*, pp. 261, 262.

16. The information is taken from Palma Guillén's Introduction to the Porrúa edition of the four volumes: see n. 7 above. (Porrúa)

17. See Jaime Quezada, Introduction to a recent edition (n.d.) of *Poema de Chile* issued by the *Casa-Museo* of Gabriela Mistral in Vicuña, p. 21. There is an extensive bibliography of her works and critical studies of her in Nuria Girona, ed,. *Gabriela Mistral: Tala, Lagar* (Cátedra: Madrid, 2001), pp. 74–83 (Cátedra).

18. It originally contained seven sections: the four listed above plus 'Childrens Verses', 'Lullabies', and a section of prose pieces. It has been re-issued in this form as *Desolación: texto completo* (Ed. Andrés Bello: Barcelona, Buenos Aires, Mexico City, Santiago, 2000). The 1922 U.S. edition was succeeded the following year by publication in Chile (Ed. Nascimento: Santiago, 1923).

19. Sources for the consideration of each of the published books include: Carmen Conde, *La obra poética de Gabriela Mistral* (EPESA: Madrid, 1970), also citing Margot Arce, Introduction to *Gabriela Mistral. Poesías completas* (Aguilar: Madrid, 1958); Erwin Haverbeck, 'El sentimiento de maternidad en *Desolación*', in *Estudios Filológicos*, No. 1 (Valdivia: Universidad Austral de Chile, 1965); Mistral's own notes to *Ternura* and *Tala*, in Porrúa pp. 106–10, 175–9;

20. *Desolación: texto completo*, p. 219.

21. Porrúa, p. 106.

22. *Ibid.*

23. *Ibid.*, p. 109.

24. The content has varied with different editions: the original (Sur: Buenos Aires, 1938) contained three sections of children's verse; these were removed from the next edition (Losada: Buenos Aires, 1947) and added to *Ternura*. The first 'complete' edition of her poems (Aguilar: Madrid, 1958, n. 19 above), followed the 1947 content, but the second revised edition (1968) added two further sections, which belong properly to the *Poema de Chile* (published privately in 1967). Cátedra *Tala* and *Lagar* (2001) reverts to the 1947 content, with the intention of presenting the book the author had approved in her lifetime.

25. As she explains in a 'Reason for this book' written for the first edition in 1938. Porrúa, p. 179.

26. The first edition (Ed. del Pacífico: Santiago, 1954) also contained children's verse, which was removed and included in *Ternura*, leaving the version included in the revised complete poems (Aguilar, 1968) shorter, also with some changes of order. This version

is followed by Cátedra. In 1991 a volume titled *Lagar II* was issued by the Directorate of Libraries, Archives, and Museums of Santiago. Its contents have been considered either a proper continuation of *Lagar*, or poems rejected by Editorial del Pacífico to keep the book to a manageable length, or poems rejected by Mistral herself. They are not included in Cátedra: see p. 73 for fuller details.

27. The South Andean huemul, *Hippocamelus bisculus*, is a small member of the camelids native to southern Chile and Argentina, now listed as endangered everywhere.

28. Cátedra, p. 68, citing Mary Louise Pratt, 'Women, Literature, and National Brotherhood', in E. Bergman *et al.*, *Women, Culture, and Politics in Latin America* Berkeley, Ca.: OUP, 1990), pp. 66, 69.

29. See Jaime Quezada, Prologue to *Poema de Chile*, pp. 23–30.

I

DESOLATION
(1922)

DESOLACIÓN

Vida

EL PENSADOR DE RODIN

A Laura Rodig

Con el mentón caído sobre la mano ruda,
el Pensador se acuerda que es carne de la huesa,
carne fatal, delante del destino desnuda,
carne que odia la muerte, y tembló de belleza.

Y tembló de amor, toda su primavera ardiente,
y ahora, al otoño, anégase de verdad y tristeza.
El "de morir tenemos" pasa sobre su frente,
en todo agudo bronce, cuando la noche empieza.

Y en la angustia, sus músculos se hienden, sufridores.
Cada surco en la carne se llena de terrores.
Se hiende, como la hoja de otoño, al Señor fuerte

que le llama en los bronces . . . Y no hay árbol torcido
de sol en la llanura, ni león de flanco herido,
crispados como este hombre que medita en la muerte.

Life

RODIN'S "THE THINKER"

For Laura Rodig

With his chin sunk down on his rough hand,
the Thinker recalls his flesh is for the grave,
doomed flesh, bare in the face of fate,
flesh quivering once in beauty and now hating death.

With love he trembled through all his burning spring,
and now, in autumn, drowns in truth and sorrow.
When night falls, shades of *memento mori*,
etched in sharp bronze, flicker across his brow.

His muscles in his torment crack with pain.
The furrows in his flesh are filled with terrors.
He cleaves, like a fallen leaf, to the strong Lord

who calls him in the bronzes . . . And no twisted tree
on the searing plain, no lion wounded in the flank,
writhes in such pain as this man dwelling on death.

AL PUEBLO HEBREO
(Matanzas de Polonia)

Raza judía, carne de dolores,
raza judía, río de amargura:
como los cielos y la tierra, dura
y crece aún, tu selva de clamores.

Nunca han dejado orearse tus heridas;
nunca han dejado que a sombrear te tiendas,
para estrujar y renovar tu venda,
más que ninguna rosa enrojecida.

Con tus gemidos se ha arrullado el mundo,
y juega con las hebras de tu llanto.
Los surcos de tu rostro, que amo tanto,
son cual llagas de sierra de profundos.

Temblando mecen su hijo las mujeres,
temblando siega el hombre su gavilla.
En tu soñar se hincó la pesadilla
y tu palabra es sólo el "¡miserere!".

Raza Judía, y aún te resta pecho
y voz de miel, para alabar tus lares,
y decir el "Cantar de los Cantares"
con lengua, y labio, y corazón deshechos.

En tu mujer camina aún María.
Sobre tu rostro va el perfil de Cristo;
por las laderas de Sión le han visto
llamarte en vano, cuando muere el día . . .

Que tu dolor en Dimas le miraba
y El dijo a Dimas la palabra inmensa,
y para ungir sus pies busca la trenza
de Magdalena ¡y la halla ensangrentada!

32

FOR THE HEBREW PEOPLE
(Massacres in Poland)

Jewish race, flesh of sorrows,
Jewish race, river of distress:
like heaven and earth, your tangle
of cries still lasts and grows louder.

They have never allowed your wounds to heal
or let you stretch out in the shade
to wring out and renew your bandages,
dyed redder than any rose.

The world has been lulled with your moans,
and it plays with the streaks of your tears.
The furrows on your face, which I so love,
are as deep as scars on a mountainside.

Trembling, women rock their babes;
shaking, men stack their sheaves.
Nightmare is rooted in your dreams,
and all you can say is *Miserere!*

Jewish race – and still you have a heart
and a honey voice with which to praise your *lares*,
reciting the Song of Solomon
with shredded tongue and lips and heart.

Mary still walks in your women;
Christ's profile fits over your face.
They have seen him on the slopes of Sion,
calling you in vain in the fading light . . .

He saw your pain in the penitent thief
and addressed him with his great word;
now he seeks the Magdalen's tress to anoint
his feet – and finds it bloodied!

¡Raza judía, carne de dolores,
raza judía, río de amargura:
como los cielos y la tierra, dura
y crece tu ancha selva de clamores!

Jewish race, flesh of sorrows,
Jewish race, river of distress:
Like heaven and earth, your broad
tangle of cries lasts and grows louder!

EL NIÑO SOLO

A Sara Hübner

Como escuchase un llanto, me paré en el repecho
y me acerqué a la puerta del rancho del camino.
Un niño de ojos dulces me miró desde el lecho
¡y una ternura inmensa me embriagó como un vino!

La madre se tardó, curvada en el barbecho;
el niño, al despertar, buscó el pezón de rosa
y rompió en llanto . . . Yo lo estreché contra el pecho,
y una canción de cuna me subió, temblorosa.

Por la ventana abierta la luna nos miraba.
El niño ya dormía, y la canción bañaba,
como otro resplandor, mi pecho enriquecido.

Y cuando la mujer, trémula, abrió la puerta,
me vería en el rostro tanta ventura cierta
¡que me dejó el infante en los brazos dormido!

THE LONE CHILD

For Sara Hübner

Thinking I heard a cry, I paused on my upward climb
and approached the door of the wayside hut.
A boy with gentle eyes stared at me from the bed,
and tenderness engulfed me like a draught of wine!

His mother was delayed, bent still over her plough;
the awakened infant, seeking her rosy nipple,
burst into sobs . . . I clasped him to my breast,
and a lullaby sprang, halting, to my lips.

Through the open window shone a watchful moon.
The boy was sleeping now, and the song suffused
my treasure-laden breast with a second shaft of light.

And when the woman opened – anxiously – the door,
the obvious happiness on my glowing face
made her leave the infant sleeping in my arms.

Dolor

BALADA

El pasó con otra;
yo le vi pasar.
Siempre dulce el viento
y el camino en paz.
¡Y estos ojos míseros
le vieron pasar!

El va amando a otra
por la tierra en flor.
Ha abierto el espino;
pasa una canción.
¡Y él va amando a otra
por la tierra en flor!

El besó a la otra
a orillas del mar;
resbaló en las olas
la luna de azahar.
¡Y no untó mi sangre
la extensión del mar!

El irá con otra
por la eternidad.
Habrá cielos dulces.
(Dios quiere callar.)
¡Y él irá con otra
por la eternidad!

Sorrow

BALLAD

He walked by with another;
I saw him pass by.
The breeze stayed gentle
and the path at peace.
And yet my wretched eyes
saw him pass by!

He goes loving another
in the flowering fields.
The hawthorn's in flower;
a song floats along.
And he's loving another
in the flowering fields!

He kissed that other
by the shore of the sea;
the orange-blossom moon
slid over the waves.
And my blood didn't tinge
the reaches of the sea!

He will go with another
till the end of time.
Skies will stay calm
(God wants to keep silent).
And he'll go with another
till the end of time!

LOS SONETOS DE LA MUERTE

I

Del nicho helado en que los hombres te pusieron,
te bajaré a la tierra humilde y soleada.
Que he de dormirme en ella los hombres no supieron,
y que hemos de soñar sobre la misma almohada.

Te acostaré en la tierra soleada con una
dulcedumbre de madre para el hijo dormido,
y la tierra ha de hacerse suavidades de cuna
al recibir tu cuerpo de niño dolorido.

Luego iré espolvoreando tierra y polvo de rosas,
y en la azulada y leve polvareda de luna,
los despojos livianos irán quedando presos.

Me alejaré cantando mis venganzas hermosas,
¡porque a ese hondor recóndito la mano de ninguna
bajará a disputarme tu puñado de huesos!

II

Este largo cansancio se hará mayor un día,
y el alma dirá al cuerpo que no quiere seguir
arrastrando su masa por la rosada vía,
por donde van los hombres, contentos de vivir.

Sentirás que a tu lado cavan briosamente,
que otra dormida llega a la quieta ciudad.
Esperaré que me hayan cubierto totalmente . . .
¡y después hablaremos por una eternidad!

Sólo entonces sabrás el por qué no madura
para las hondas huesas tu carne todavía,
tuviste que bajar, sin fatiga, a dormir.

THE SONNETS OF DEATH

1

From the frozen niche in which men laid you
I shall take you down to humble, sunlit ground.
That I should sleep there too they did not know,
nor that we should dream on the same pillow.

I shall tuck you tenderly into the sunlit earth
with a mother's touch for her sleeping son,
and the earth will take on the softness of a cradle
when it receives your body of a wounded child.

Then I shall scatter earth and powdered roses,
whose light remains will be imprisoned
in the thin blue dust-cloud lit by the moon.

I shall depart giving voice to my lovely revenges,
because at these hidden depths no other woman's hand
will reach down to contend for your fistful of bones!

2

This endless weariness will grow worse one day,
and the soul will tell the body it doesn't want to go on
dragging its mass along that rosy road
down which men go, content to be alive.

You will feel them determinedly digging beside you,
that another sleeping woman has reached the silent city.
I shall wait until they have covered me completely . . .
And then we shall talk till the end of time!

Only then will you learn why, your flesh
not ready yet for the deep graves,
you had to descend, effortlessly, into sleep.

Se hará luz en la zona de los sinos, oscura;
sabrás que en nuestra alianza signo de astros había
y, roto el pacto enorme, tenías que morir.

III

Malas manos tomaron tu vida desde el día
en que, a una señal de astros, dejara su plantel
nevado de azucenas. En gozo florecía.
Malas manos entraron trágicamente en él . . .

Y yo dije al Señor: – "Por las sendas mortales
le llevan. ¡Sombra amada que no saben guiar!
¡Arráncalo, Señor, a esas manos fatales
o le hundes en el largo sueño que sabes dar!

¡No le puedo gritar, no le puedo seguir!
Su barca empuja un negro viento de tempestad.
Retórnalo a mis brazos o le siegas en flor".

Se detuvo la barca rosa de su vivir . . .
¿Que no sé del amor, que no tuve piedad?
¡Tú, que vas a juzgarme, lo comprendes, Señor!

Light will creep into the dark zone of the fates;
you will know our alliance was in our star signs,
and once that great pact was broken, you had to die.

3

Wicked hands took hold of your life from the day
when its nursery bed, at a sign from the heavens,
was snow-clad in lilies. Joy made it bloom.
Evil hands then made their fateful entrance . . .

And I told the Lord: "They are taking him down deathly
paths – the beloved shade they know not how to guide!
Snatch him back, Lord, from those deadly hands
or sink him in the long sleep you know how to give!

I cannot cry out to him, cannot run after him!
A stormy black wind drives his boat onward.
Bring him back to my arms or you'll cut short his life!"

Then the rosy boat of his lifetime slowed to a stop . . .
I don't know how to love? I showed him no mercy?
You, Lord, who will judge me: you know how it was!

EL RUEGO

Señor, tú sabes cómo, con encendido brío,
por los seres extraños mi palabra te invoca.
Vengo ahora a pedirte por uno que era mío,
mi vaso de frescura, el panal de mi boca,

cal de mis huesos, dulce razón de la jornada,
gorjeo de mi oído, ceñidor de mi veste.
Me cuido hasta de aquéllos en que no puse nada;
¡no tengas ojo torvo si te pido por éste!

Te digo que era bueno, te digo que tenía
el corazón entero a flor de pecho, que era
suave de índole, franco como la luz del día,
henchido de milagro como la primavera.

Me replicas, severo, que es de plegaria indigno
el que no untó de preces sus dos labios febriles,
y se fue aquella tarde sin esperar tu signo,
trizándose las sienes como vasos sutiles.

Pero yo, mi Señor, te arguyo que he tocado,
de la misma manera que el nardo de su frente,
todo su corazón dulce y atormentado
¡y tenía la seda del capullo naciente!

¿Que fue cruel? Olvidas, Señor, que le quería,
y el sabía suya la entraña que llagaba.
¿Que enturbió para siempre mis linfas de alegría?
¡No importa! Tú comprende: ¡yo le amaba, le amaba!

Y amar (bien sabes de eso) es amargo ejercicio;
un mantener los párpados de lágrimas mojados,
un refrescar de besos las trenzas del cilicio
conservando, bajo ellas, los ojos extasiados.

El hierro que taladra tiene un gustoso frío,
cuando abre, cual gavillas, las carnes amorosas.

PRAYER

Lord, you know with what heartfelt concern
I've invoked your help for the needs of strangers.
Now I come to plead for one who was mine,
my draught of freshness, honey to my lips.

Marrow of my bones, sweet reason through my day,
birdsong to my ears, sash to gird my robe.
I care even for those I've never known:
don't you look sternly on my pleas for him!

I tell you he was good, that he wore
his whole heart on his sleeve, that he was
gentle by nature, frank as the daylight,
bursting with the miracles of spring.

You reply, sternly, he's not worthy of my plea,
since his two fevered lips were never dabbed with prayer,
since he left one evening, not waiting for your sign,
shattering his temples like the finest vase.

But, my Lord, I put it to you that I caressed
the whole of his gentle yet tormented heart,
as I did the spikenard of his smooth brow –
and it had the silky softness of an opening bud!

So he was cruel? You forget, Lord, that I loved him,
that he knew he owned the bowels he wounded.
So he stained the pure pool of my joy for ever?
So what? You must realize: I loved him, loved him!

And loving (as you will know) is a bitter business;
it means eyelids always wet with running tears,
cooling your thorn-crowned hair with kisses
while beneath it your eyes must still look ecstatic.

The piercing iron has a welcoming coldness
as it opens loving flesh like sheaves.

45

Y la cruz (Tú te acuerdas ¡oh Rey de los judíos!)
se lleva con blandura, como un gajo de rosas.

Aquí me estoy, Señor, con la cara caída
sobre el polvo, parlándote un crepúsculo entero,
o todos los crepúsculos a que alcance la vida,
si tardas en decirme la palabra que espero.

Fatigaré tu oído de preces y sollozos,
lamiendo, lebrel tímido, los bordes de tu manto,
y ni pueden huirme tus ojos amorosos
ni esquivar tu piel el riego caliente de mi llanto.

¡Di el perdón, dilo al fin! Va a esparcir en el viento
la palabra el perfume de cien pomos de olores
al vaciarse; toda agua será deslumbramiento;
el yermo echará flor y el guijarro esplendores.

Se mojarán los ojos oscuros de las fieras,
y, comprendiendo, el monte que de piedra forjaste
llorará por los párpados blancos de sus neveras:
¡toda la tierra tuya sabrá que perdonaste!

And the cross (as you remember, King of the Jews!)
is light to carry, like a bunch of roses.

So here I am now, Lord, my face prostrated
in the dust, speaking to you one whole evening –
or for all the evenings that my life may span
if you won't give me the word for which I long.

I shall wear out your ears with prayer and sobs,
a shy greyhound licking the hem of your cloak,
and neither can your loving eyes ignore me,
nor your skin escape the hot sprinkle of my tears.

Forgive him, finally! Your word will scatter
the scent from a hundred bottles to the wind
and as they empty, all water will be dazzling,
the wilderness will bloom and boulders glow.

The eyes of wild beasts will be wet with tears,
and, understanding, the peaks you forge of stone
will weep through the white eyelids of their snow:
this whole earth of yours will know that you forgave him!

LOS HUESOS DE LOS MUERTOS

Los huesos de los muertos
hielo sutil saben espolvorear
sobre las bocas de los que quisieron.
¡Y éstas no pueden nunca más besar!

Los huesos de los muertos
en paletadas echan su blancor
sobre la llama intensa de la vida.
¡Le matan todo ardor!

Los huesos de los muertos
pueden más que la carne de los vivos.
Aun desgajados hacen eslabones
fuertes, donde nos tienen sumisos y cautivos!

THE BONES OF THE DEAD

The bones of the dead
know how to sprinkle fine ice
on the mouths of those they loved.
And these lips can no longer kiss!

The bones of the dead
spread their whiteness in spadefulls
over the ardent flame of life,
killing all its passion!

The bones of the dead
are stronger than living flesh.
Even broken, they make strong shackles
to keep us subject and imprisoned!

Naturaleza

A Don Juan Contardi

PAISAJES DE LA PATAGONIA

I. DESOLACION

La bruma espesa, eterna, para que olvide dónde
me ha arrojado la mar en su ola de salmuera.
La tierra a la que vine no tiene primavera:
tiene su noche larga que cual madre me esconde.

El viento hace a mi casa su ronda de sollozos
y de alarido, y quiebra, como un cristal. mi grito.
Y en la llanura blanca, de horizonte infinito,
miro morir inmensos ocasos dolorosos.

¿A quién podrá llamar la que hasta aquí ha venido
si más lejos que ella sólo fueron los muertos?
¡Tan sólo ellos contemplan un mar callado y yerto
crecer entre sus brazos y los brazos queridos!

Los barcos cuyas velas blanquean en el puerto
vienen de tierras donde no están los que son míos;
sus hombres de ojos claros no conocen mis ríos
y traen frutos pálidos, sin la luz de mis huertos.

Y la interrogación que sube a mi garganta
al mirarlos pasar, me desciende, vencida:
hablan extrañas lenguas y no la conmovida
lengua que en tierras de oro mi vieja madre canta.

Miro bajar la nieve como el polvo en la huesa;
miro crecer la niebla como el agonizante,
y por no enloquecer no cuento los instantes,
porque la *noche larga* ahora tan sólo empieza.

Nature

For Don Juan Contardi

PATAGONIAN LANDSCAPES

I. DESOLATION

The fog is thick and endless, making me forget
where the sea hurled me on its briny waves.
The land I came to has no spring; it has
its long night that enfolds me like a mother.

The wind prowls round my house, sobbing, shrieking,
and shatters my shout like a window-pane.
And I see vast sorrowing sunsets die
in the infinite depths of the snow-clad plain.

Once come this far, to whom can she call,
if beyond her lie only the dead?
They alone watch a silent, stiff sea swell
between their arms and those of their loved ones!

The ships with bleached sails in the harbour
come from lands where my people do not dwell;
their bright-eyed men have never seen my rivers,
and they bring pale fruits, lacking my orchards' light.

And the questions that rise up in my throat
when I see them pass, subside, defeated:
they speak in strange tongues, not in the stirring tones
of my aged mother's songs in her gold-lit land.

I watch the snow fall like dust on a grave;
I watch the mist rise like a man on his death-bed,
and I don't count the minutes for fear of going mad,
knowing the long night on which I now embark.

Miro el llano extasiado y recojo su duelo,
que vine para ver los paisajes mortales.
La nieve es el semblante que asoma a mis cristales;
¡siempre será su albura bajando de los cielos!

Siempre ella, silenciosa, como la gran mirada
de Dios sobre mí; siempre su azahar sobre mi casa;
siempre, como el destino que ni mengua ni pasa,
descenderá a cubrirme, terrible y extasiada.

II. ARBOL MUERTO

A Alberto Guillén

En el medio del llano,
un árbol seco su blasfemia alarga;
un árbol blanco, roto
y mordido de llagas,
en el que el viento, vuelto
ni desesperación, aúlla y pasa.

De su bosque, el que ardió, sólo dejaron
de escarnio, su fantasma.
Una llama alcanzó hasta su costado
y lo lamió, como el amor mi alma.
¡Y sube de la herida un purpurino
musgo, como una estrofa ensangrentada!

Los que amó, y que ceñían
a su torno en septiembre una guirnalda,
cayeron. Sus raíces
los buscan, torturadas,
tanteando por el césped
con una angustia humana.

Le dan los plenilunios en el llano
sus más mortales platas,
y alargan, por que mida su amargura,

I look over the enraptured plain and take in its sorrow –
it was landscapes of death that I came here to see.
The snow is the spectre looking in at my windows;
its perfect whiteness always falling from the skies!

Always this whiteness: silent, like the great gaze of God
on me; as though covering my house with orange-blossom,
never waning nor ceasing, terrifying yet ecstatic,
falling for ever, fate's blanket to cover my tomb.

II. DEAD TREE

For Alberto Guillén

Out on the plain a dead tree
brandishes its blasphemy;
a whitened tree, split
and scarred with its wounds,
through which the wind, become
my desperation, howls and tears.

It was a wood that caught fire,
leaving just its taunting ghost.
A flame reached up its side
and licked it, as love did my soul.
And the wound is filled with moss,
purplish as a blood-stained verse!

Those it loved, who in September
tied a garland round its trunk,
have fallen. Now its tortured
roots seek for them,
probing the grassy ground
in palpably human pain.

The full moon lights the plain
with its most deadly silvers,
and its desolate shadows stretch out

hasta lejos su sombra desolada.
¡Y él le da al pasajero
su atroz blasfemia y su visión amarga!

III. TRES ARBOLES

Tres árboles caídos
quedaron a la orilla del sendero.
El leñador los olvidó, y conversan,
apretados de amor, como tres ciegos.

El sol de ocaso pone
su sangre viva en los hendidos leños
¡y se llevan los vientos la fragancia
de su costado abierto!

Uno, torcido, tiende
su brazo inmenso y de follaje trémulo
hacia otro, y sus heridas
como dos ojos son, llenos de ruego.

El leñador los olvidó. La noche
vendrá. Estaré con ellos.
Recibiré en mi corazón sus mansas
resinas. Me serán como de fuego.
¡Y mudos y ceñidos,
nos halle el día en un montón de duelo!

to the measure of its bitterness.
And from it the traveller takes on
its awful curse and bitter prophecy!

3. THREE TREES

Three fallen trees
left by the side of the path
by a forgetful woodman, converse
like three blind men, bound in love.

The setting sun tinges
their split limbs with bright blood,
and the winds bear the scent
of their open sides!

One, twisted, holds out
its great branch with trembling leaves
towards another, and their wounds
are like two eyes, asking for mercy.

Forgotten by the woodman – night
will come. I shall be with them.
Their gentle resins will infuse
my heart. They will be my fire.
And so let morning find us
silent and cuddled in a heap of sorrow.

A LAS NUBES

Nubes vaporosas,
nubes como tul,
llevad l'alma mía
por el cielo azul.

¡Lejos de la casa
que me ve sufrir,
lejos de estos muros
que me ven morir!

Nubes pasajeras,
llevadme hacia el mar,
a escuchar el canto
de la pleamar
y entre la guirnalda
de olas a cantar.

Nubes, flores, rostros,
dibujadme a aquél
que ya va borrándose
por el tiempo infiel.
Mi alma se pudre
sin el rostro de él.

Nubes que pasáis,
nubes, detened
sobre el pecho mío
la fresca merced.
¡Abiertos están
mis labios de sed!

TO THE CLOUDS

Ethereal clouds,
clouds made of tulle,
carry my soul
through the blue sky.

Far from the house
that sees me suffer,
far from these walls
that watch me die!

Fleeting clouds,
take me to the sea,
to hear the song
of high tide
and to sing amid
the garland of waves.

Clouds, flowers, faces:
portray me the one
who is growing dim
with faithless time.
My soul is decaying
from not seeing his face.

You clouds that pass by,
hold back to pour
your fresh mercy
on my breast.
My open lips are
burning with thirst!

OTOÑO

A esta alameda muriente
he traído mi cansancio,
y estoy ya no sé qué tiempo
tendida bajo los álamos,
que van cubriendo mi pecho
de su oro divino y tardo.

Sin un ímpetu la tarde
se apagó tras de los álamos.
Por mi corazón mendigo
ella no se ha ensangrentado.
Y el amor al que tendí,
para salvarme, los brazos
se está muriendo en mi alma
como arrebol desflocado.

Y no llevaba más que este
manojito atribulado
de ternura, entre mis carnes
como un infante, temblando.
¡Ahora se me va perdiendo
como un agua entre los álamos;
pero es otoño, y no agito,
para salvarlo, mis brazos.

En mis sienes la hojarasca
exhala un perfume manso.
Tal vez morir sólo sea
ir con asombro marchando
entre un rumor de hojas secas
y por un parque extasiado.

Aunque va a llegar la noche,
y estoy sola, y ha blanqueado
el suelo un azahar de escarcha,
para regresar no me alzo,
ni hago lecho entre las hojas,

AUTUMN

To this stand of autumn poplars
I have brought my fatigue
and – for how many hours?–
lain under its trees,
which are covering my breast
with their heavenly slow gold.

With no rush, evening has
faded behind the poplars.
It has failed to turn blood-red
for my begging heart.
And the love to which, to save myself,
I held out my arms
is dying away in my soul
like a fading sunset cloud.

And all I carried was this
tiny afflicted handful
of tenderness that trembled
like an infant within my flesh.
And now it is slipping from me
like water through the poplars,
but it is autumn, and I do not wave
my arms to keep it back.

On my temples the dead leaves
breathe a gentle perfume.
Perhaps dying means no more
than walking astounded
through the rustle of dry leaves
and in an enchanted park.

Although night is falling and I am alone,
and even though the ground
is bleached by an orange-blossom frost,
I don't rise to return
or make myself a bed among the leaves;

ni acierto a dar, sollozando,
un inmenso Padre Nuestro
por mi inmenso desamparo!

Figure 10. Vicuña today: Calle Gabriela Mistral from the Casa-Museo

nor can I utter
a vast sobbing Our Father to match
my limitless desolation.

Figure 11. Vicuña: G.M.'s family home at the Casa-Museo (reconstruction), exterior

CIMA

La hora de la tarde, la que pone
su sangre en las montañas.

Alguien en esta hora está sufriendo;
una pierde, angustiada,
en este atardecer el solo pecho
contra el cual estrechaba.

Hay algún corazón en donde moja
la tarde aquella cima ensangrentada.

El valle ya está en sombra
y se llena de calma.
Pero mira de lo hondo que se enciende
de rojez la montaña.

Yo me pongo a cantar siempre a esta hora
mi invariable canción atribulada.
¿Seré yo la que baño
la cumbre de escarlata?

Llevo a mi corazón la mano, y siento
que mi costado mana.

SUMMIT

The evening hour, which sets
its blood upon the mountain.

Someone is suffering at this hour;
in this dusk an anguished woman
is losing the only heart to which
she ever pressed herself.

There is some heart in which evening
steeps that blooded summit.

The valley is now in shadow
and is filled with peace.
But from its depths she sees
the mountain blazing red.

At this hour I always start singing
my single song of tribulation.
Shall I be the one bathing
the summit in scarlet?

I place my hand on my heart
and feel the flow from my side.

Figure 12. Vicuña: G.M.'s family home, interior

II

TENDERNESS
(1924)

TERNURA

Canciones de Cuna

MECIENDO

El mar sus millares de olas
mece, divino.
Oyendo a los mares amantes,
mezo a mi niño.

El viento errabundo en la noche
mece los trigos.
Oyendo a los vientos amantes,
mezo a mi niño.

Dios Padre sus miles de mundos
mece sin ruido.
Sintiendo su mano en la sombra
mezo a mi niño.

Lullabies

ROCKING

The divine sea rocks
its myriad waves.
To the sound of the loving seas
I rock my child.

The wind roaming in the night
ruffles the wheat fields.
To the sound of the loving winds
I rock my child.

God the Father, silently,
rocks his myriad worlds.
To the touch of his hand in the dark
I rock my child.

HALLAZGO

Me encontré este niño
cuando al campo iba:
dormido lo he hallado
en unas espigas . . .

O tal vez ha sido
cruzando la viña:
buscando los pámpanos
topé su mejilla.

Y por eso temo,
al quedar dormida,
se evapore como
la helada en las viñas.

DISCOVERY

I came upon this boy
on my way to the fields:
I found him asleep
among the wheat ears . . .

Or perhaps it was while
I was crossing the vineyard:
feeling for tendrils,
I brushed his cheek.

And so I fear
as I fall asleep,
he'll melt away
like frost on the vines.

NIÑO MEXICANO

Estoy en donde no estoy,
en el Anáhuac plateado,
y en su luz como no hay otra
peino un niño de mis manos.

En mis rodillas parece
flecha caída del arco,
y como flecha lo afilo
meciéndolo y canturreando.

En luz tan vieja y tan niña
siempre me parece hallazgo,
y lo mudo y lo volteo
con el refrán que le canto.

Me miran con vida eterna
sus ojos negri-azulados,
y como en costumbre eterna,
yo lo peino de mis manos.

Resinas de pino-ocote
van de su nuca a mis brazos,
y es pesado y es ligero
de ser la flecha sin arco . . .

Lo alimento con un ritmo,
y él me nutre de algún bálsamo
que es el bálsamo del maya
del que a mí me despojaron.

Yo juego con sus cabellos
y los abro y los repaso,
y en sus cabellos recobro
a los mayas dispersados.

Hace doce años dejé
a mi niño mexicano;

MEXICAN CHILD

I am where I am not,
on the silvery Anáhuac,
and by its light like no other
I comb a child's hair with my hands.

On my knees he looks like
an arrow fallen from a bow,
and I sharpen him like an arrow
rocking him and singing softly.

In a light so old and so young,
he will always be my find,
and I change him and turn him
with the refrain I sing.

His blue-black eyes gaze up at me
with everlasting life,
and in the age-old gesture
I comb him with my hands.

From his nape to my arms
flow resins of torch-pine,
and he is both heavy and light,
being an arrow without a bow . . .

I feed him at regular hours,
and he nourishes me with balm,
the balsam of the Maya,
which they took away from me.

I play with his hair,
part it and smooth it,
and in it I find once again
the scattered Mayan people.

It is twelve years since I let
my little Mexican boy go;

pero despierta o dormida
yo lo peino de mis manos . . .

¡Es una maternidad
que no me cansa el regazo,
y es un éxtasis que tengo
de la gran muerte librado!

but whether I'm awake or asleep,
I comb him with my hands.

This is a motherhood
that never weighs down my lap,
an enchantment I possess,
rescued from great death!

Rondas

TIERRA CHILENA

Danzamos en tierra chilena,
más bella que Lía y Raquel;
la tierra que amasa a los hombres
de labios y pecho sin hiel . . .

La tierra más verde de huertos,
la tierra más rubia de mies,
la tierra más roja de viñas,
¡qué dulce que roza los pies!

Su polvo hizo nuestras mejillas,
su río, nuestro reír,
y besa los pies de la ronda
que la hace cual madre gemir.

Es bella, y por bella queremos
sus pastos de rondas albear;
es libre y por libre deseamos
su rostro de cantos bañar.

Mañana abriremos sus rocas,
la haremos viñedo y pomar;
mañana alzaremos sus pueblos
¡hoy sólo queremos danzar!

Rounds

CHILEAN LAND

We dance on Chilean land,
more lovely than Lea or Rachel;
the land that kneads men
with lips and heart without gall . . .

The greenest land of orchards,
the fairest land of grain
the reddest land of vineyards –
how gently it brushes our feet!

Its dust formed our cheeks,
its river made our laughter,
and it kisses the feet of the dancers,
making it moan like a mother.

It is lovely, and its loveliness makes us
want to light up its fields in our dance;
it is free, and its freedom inspires us
to want to bathe its face in our songs.

Tomorrow we shall open its rocks;
we shall turn it to vineyard and orchard;
tomorrow we shall build its towns –
today we just want to dance!

La Desvariadora

MIEDO

Yo no quiero que a mi niña
golondrina me la vuelvan.
Se hunde volando en el cielo
y no baja hasta mi estera;
en el alero hace nido
y mis manos no la peinan.
Yo no quiero que a mi niña
golondrina me la vuelvan.

Yo no quiero que a mi niña
la vayan a hacer princesa.
Con zapatitos de oro
¿cómo juega en las praderas?
Y cuando llegue la noche
a mi lado no se acuesta . . .
Yo no quiero que a mi niña
la vayan a hacer princesa.

Y menos quiero que un día
me la vayan a hacer reina.
La pondrían en un trono
a donde mis pies no llegan.
Cuando viniese la noche
yo no podría mecerla . . .
¡Yo no quiero que a mi niña
me la vayan a hacer reina!

The Nonsense Rhymer

FEAR

I do not want them to turn
my girl into a swallow –
flying to immerse herself in heaven
and never coming down to my mat.
She nests way up in the eaves
and I can't run my hands through her hair.
I do not want them to turn
my girl into a swallow.

I do not want them to make
my girl into a princess.
In tiny golden slippers,
how can she play in the fields?
And when night comes she will not
be lying next to me . . .
I do not want them to make
my girl into a princess.

Still less do I want them one day
to go and make her queen.
They would put her up on a throne
out of reach of my feet.
And when night came I could
no longer rock her to sleep . . .
I don't want them to take my girl
and go and make her queen!

Jugarretas

LA RATA

Una rata corrió a un venado
y los venados al jaguar,
y los jaguares a los búfalos,
y los búfalos a la mar.

¡Pillen, pillen a los que se van!
¡Pillen a la rata, pillen al venado,
pillen a los búfalos y a la mar!

Miren que la rata de la delantera
se lleva en las patas lana de bordar,
y con la lana bordo mi vestido
y con el vestido me voy a casar.

Suban y pasen la llanada,
corran sin aliento, sigan sin parar,
vuelen por la novia, y por el cortejo,
y por la carroza y el velo nupcial.

Bad Moves

THE RAT

A rat ran after a deer,
the deer ran after a jaguar,
the jaguar after the buffaloes,
and the buffaloes after the sea.

Catch, catch them running away!
Catch the rat, catch the deer,
catch the buffaloes and the sea!

Look at the rat out in front
carrying yarn in its paws;
with that yarn I'll trim my dress,
and in that dress I'll marry.

Up and over the plain you go
out of breath, go on, don't stop.
Fly for the bride and the wedding guests,
for the carriage and the bridal veil!

Cuenta-Mundo

EL AIRE

Esto que pasa y que se queda,
esto es el Aire, esto es el Aire,
y sin boca que tú le veas
te toma y besa, padre amante.
¡Ay, le rompemos sin romperle;
herido vuela sin quejarse,
y parece que a todos lleva
y a todos deja, por buenos, el Aire . . .

World-tale

THE AIR

This thing that is gone yet still here,
this is the Air, this is the Air,
and without a mouth that you can see
it takes and kisses you, a loving father.
Alas! We break it without it breaking;
it flies off wounded but uncomplaining,
and it seems that the Air
takes and leaves everyone for good . . .

MONTAÑA

Hijo mío, tú subirás
con el ganado a la Montaña.
Pero mientras yo te arrebato
y te llevo sobre mi espalda.

Apuñada y negra la vemos,
como mujer enfurruñada.
Vive sola de todo tiempo,
pero nos ama, la Montaña,
y hace señales de subir
tirando gestos con que llama . . .

Trepamos, hijo, los faldeos,
llenos de robles y de hayas.
Arremolina el viento hierbas
y balancea la Montaña,
y van los brazos de tu madre
abriendo moños que son zarzas . . .

Mirando al llano, que está ciego,
ya no vemos río ni casa.
Pero tu madre sabe subir,
perder la Tierra, y volver salva.

Pasan las nieblas en trapos rotos;
se borra el mundo cuando pasan.
Subimos tanto que ya no quieres
seguir y todo te sobresalta.
Pero del alto Pico del Toro,
nadie desciende a la llanada.

El sol, lo mismo que el faisán,
de una vez salta la Montaña,
y de una vez baña de oro
a la Tierra que era fantasma,
¡y le enseña gajo por gajo
en redonda fruta mondada!

MOUNTAIN

My son, you will ascend
the Mountain with the flock.
But only if I snatch you up
and carry you on my back.

Kneaded and black she looks,
like a disgruntled woman.
She has always lived alone,
but the Mountain truly loves us
and invites us to climb her flanks,
making summoning signs . . .

We clamber, son, over her skirts
full of oak trees and beeches.
The wind makes whorls in the grasses,
and the Mountain sways,
while your mother's arms push
through thickets of brambles . . .

Looking down on the plain, now blind,
we see neither river nor house.
But your mother knows how to climb,
to lose the Earth, and come back safe.

Mists roll by in torn-up rags,
rubbing out the world as they pass.
We climb so high you now don't want
to go on, and everything startles you.
But from the high Bull's Peak
no one goes down to the plain.

The sun, just like the pheasant,
leaps the mountain in one bound,
and at a stroke bathes in gold
the Earth that was a ghost,
and segment by segment reveals it
to be a round peeled fruit!

ALONDRAS

Bajaron a mancha de trigo,
y al acercarnos, voló la banda,
y la alameda se quedó
del azoro como rasgada.

En matorrales parecen fuego;
cuando suben, plata lanzada,
y pasan antes de que pasen,
y te rebanan la alabanza.

Saben no más los pobres ojos
que pasó toda la bandada,
y gritando llaman "¡alondras!"
a lo que sube, se pierde y canta.

Y en este aire malherido
nos han dejado llenos de ansia,
con el asombro y el temblor
a mitad del cuerpo y el alma . . .

¡Alondras, hijo, nos cruzamos
las alondras, por la llanada!

LARKS

They descended on a patch of wheat
and flew away at our approach,
and the poplar grove was left
torn with the tumult.

In the scrub, they look like fire;
when they rise, darting silver,
and they pass by in a flash,
slicing through our words of praise.

Out poor eyes know only
that the whole flock is gone;
and with a shout we call out "Larks!"
as they rise and vanish with their song.

And in this sorely injured air
they have left us filled with longing,
with amazement and a shiver
in the heart of our body and soul . . .

Larks, son, we came upon
the larks, out there on the plain!

LA TIERRA

Niño indio, si estás cansado,
tú te acuestas sobre la Tierra,
y lo mismo si estás alegre,
hijo mío, juega con ella . . .

Se oyen cosas maravillosas
al tambor indio de la Tierra:
se oye el fuego que sube y baja
buscando el cielo, y no sosiega.
Rueda y rueda, se oyen los ríos
en cascadas que no se cuentan.
Se oyen mugir los animales;
se oye el hacha comer la selva.
Se oyen sonar telares indios.
Se oyen trillas, se oyen fiestas.

Donde el indio lo está llamando,
el tambor indio le contesta,
y tañe cerca y tañe lejos,
como el que huye y que regresa . . .

Todo lo toma, todo lo carga
el lomo santo de la Tierra:
lo que camina, lo que duerme,
lo que retoza y lo que pena;
y lleva vivos y lleva muertos
el tambor indio de la Tierra.

Cuando muera, no llores, hijo:
Pecho a pecho ponte con ella,
y si sujetas los alientos
como que todo o nada fueras,
tú escucharás subir su brazo
que me tenía y que me entrega,
y la madre que estaba rota
tú la verás volver entera.

THE EARTH

Indian child, if you are tired,
you lie down upon the Earth,
and do the same if you are happy:
my son, play with her . . .

The Indian drum of the earth
tells of wonderful things:
you hear fire rising and falling,
seeking the sky, never resting.
In roll upon roll you hear rivers
falling in countless cascades.
You hear the animals bellow;
you hear the axe eat the forest.
You hear Indian looms ringing;
you hear threshing and feasting.

Wherever Indians summon it,
the Indian drum replies;
it beats near and it beats far,
like someone fleeing and returning . . .

Everything is carried, everything borne
on the holy back of the Earth:
all that walks, all that sleeps,
all that gambols and all that suffers;
and the Indian drum of the Earth
carries off living and dead.

When I die, don't cry, my son:
stretch yourself face down on her,
and if you hold your breath,
as if you were all or nothing,
you will hear her raise her arm,
which held me and gives me back,
and you will see the mother
that was broken return whole.

III

FELLING
(1938)

TALA

Muerte de mi Madre

LA FUGA

Madre mía, en el sueño
ando por paisajes cardenosos:
un monte negro que se contornea
siempre, para alcanzar el otro monte;
y en el que sigue estás tú vagamente,
pero siempre hay otro monte redondo
que circundar, para pagar el paso
al monte de tu gozo y de mi gozo.

Mas, a trechos tú misma vas haciendo
el camino de juegos y de expolios.
Vamos las dos sintiéndonos, sabiéndonos,
mas no podemos vernos en los ojos,
y no podemos trocarnos palabra,
cual la Eurídice y el Orfeo solos,
las dos cumpliendo un voto o un castigo,
ambas con pies y con acentos rotos.

Pero a veces no vas al lado mío:
te llevo en mí, en un peso angustioso
y amoroso a la vez, como pobre hijo
galeoto a su padre galeoto,
y hay que enhebrar los cerros repetidos,
sin decir el secreto doloroso:
que yo te llevo hurtada a dioses crueles
y que vamos a un Dios que es de nosotros.

Y otras veces ni estás cerro adelante,
ni vas conmigo, ni vas en mi soplo:
te has disuelto con niebla en las montañas,
te has cedido al paisaje cardenoso.
Y me das unas voces de sarcasmo
desde tres puntos, y en dolor me rompo,
porque mi cuerpo es uno, el que me diste,

Death of my Mother

FLIGHT

Dear mother, in my dream
I walk through livid landscapes:
a black mountain whose profile is always
stretching to reach the next mountain;
and in the next one you are vaguely there,
but there is always another humped mountain
to encompass, to pay for the passage
to the mountain of your joy and my joy.

Yet at times you yourself are making
the path with ploys and deceits.
We two move on, sensing and knowing each other,
but we can't see one another in our eyes,
and, alone like Eurydice and Orpheus,
we cannot exchange a word,
both serving out an oath or a sentence,
both of us with broken feet and voices.

But sometimes you walk no longer by my side:
I carry you inside me, like a poor son
pimping for his pimping father,
as a painful weight, yet loving,
and I have to thread successive hills
without revealing the painful secret:
that I bear you stolen from cruel gods,
and we go to a God who is our God.

And other times you are no longer one hill ahead,
nor are you in my breath: nor with me are you going,
you have dissolved with the mountain mist,
and the livid landscape has engulfed you.
And you speak sarcastic words to me
from three directions, and I am seized with sorrow,
because I have just one body, the one you gave me,

y tú eres un agua de cien ojos,
y eres un paisaje de mil brazos,
nunca más lo que son los amorosos:
un pecho vivo sobre un pecho vivo
nudo de bronce ablandado en sollozo.

Y nunca estamos, nunca nos quedamos,
como dicen que quedan los gloriosos,
delante de su Dios, en dos anillos
de luz, o en dos medallones absortos,
ensartados en un rayo de gloria
o acostados en un cauce de oro.

O te busco, y no sabes que te busco,
o vas conmigo, y no te veo el rostro;
o en mí tú vas, en terrible convenio;
sin responderme con tu cuerpo sordo,
siempre por el rosario de los cerros,
que cobran sangre por entregar gozo,
y hacen danzar en torno a cada uno,
¡hasta el momento de la sien ardiendo,
del cascabel de la antigua demencia
y de la trampa en el vórtice rojo!

while you are water with a hundred eyes of pools,
you are a landscape with a thousand arms,
never more to be the stuff of lovers:
a living breast upon a living breast,
a knot of bronze dissolving into sobs.

And we never stand, and never stay,
as they say do those who are in glory,
before their God, in two rings of light
or two medallions, absorbed,
strung together in a ray of glory,
or lying in a stream of gold.

Either I seek you, without your knowing my quest,
or, without my seeing your face, with me you go;
or you travel within me, in a terrible pact,
without answering me with your deaf body,
all along the rosary of the hills,
which charge blood for granting joy,
and make each one dance in turn
until the moment of the burning brow,
of the rattling of the ancient madness,
and of the trap in the scarlet vortex!

Alucinación

LA ROSA

La riqueza del centro de la rosa
es la riqueza de tu corazón.
Desátala como ella:
su ceñidura es toda tu aflicción.

Desátala en un canto
o en un tremendo amor.
No defiendas la rosa:
¡te quemaría con el resplandor!

Hallucination

THE ROSE

The riches of the heart of the rose
are like the wealth of your heart.
Let them out as it does:
holding them in is all your pain.

Let them out in a song
or in a great love.
Don't shield the rose:
it would scorch you with its glare.

Saudade

LA EXTRANJERA
A Francis de Miomandre

"Habla con dejo de sus mares bárbaros,
con no sé qué algas y no sé qué arenas;
reza oración a dios sin bulto y peso,
envejecida como si muriera.
En huerto nuestro que nos hizo extraño,
ha puesto cactus y zarpadas hierbas.
Alienta del resuello del desierto
y ha amado con pasión de que blanquea,
que nunca cuenta y que si nos contase
sería como el mapa de otra estrella.
Vivirá entre nosotros ochenta años,
pero siempre será como si llega
hablando lengua que jadea y gime
y que le entienden sólo bestezuelas.
Y va a morirse en medio de nosotros,
en una noche en la que más padezca,
con sólo su destino por almohada,
de una muerte callada y *extranjera*".

Nostalgia

THE FOREIGNER
For Francis de Miomandre

"She speaks with a trace of her barbarous seas
with their unknown seaweeds and unknown sands;
she prays to a formless and weightless God,
grown as old as if she were dying.
In our orchard she has made strange to us
she has planted cactus and saw-grass.
A wind from the desert gives her breath,
and she has loved with a passion that blanches her,
a love she never tells and, if she told us,
would be like the map of another star.
She will dwell among us for eighty years,
but it will always be like when she came
speaking her heaving and groaning tongue
that dumb beasts alone understand.
And she is going to die in our midst,
on the night of her greatest suffering,
with only her fate for a pillow,
of a silent and *foreign* death."

BEBER
Al Dr Pedro de Alba

Recuerdo gestos de criaturas
y son gestos de darme el agua.

En el Valle de Río Blanco,
en donde nace el Aconcagua,
llegué a beber, salté a beber
en el fuete de una cascada,
que caía crinada y dura
y se rompía yerta y blanca.
Pegué mi boca al hervidero,
y me quemaba el agua santa,
y tres días sangró mi boca
de aquel sorbo del Aconcagua.

En el campo de Mitla, un día
de cigarras, de sol, de marcha,
me doblé a un pozo y vino un indio
a sostenerme sobre el agua,
y mi cabeza, como un fruto,
estaba dentro de sus palmas.
Bebía yo lo que bebía,
que era su cara con mi cara,
y en un relámpago yo supe
carne de Mitla ser mi casta.

En la Isla de Puerto Rico,
a la siesta de azul colmada,
mi cuerpo quieto, las olas locas,
y como cien madres las palmas,
rompió una niña por donaire
junto a mi boca un coco de agua,
y yo bebí, como una hija,
agua de madre, agua de palma.
Y más dulzura no he bebido
con el cuerpo ni con el alma.

DRINKING
For Dr Pedro de Alba

I recall gestures of young children,
and they are gestures of giving me water.

In the valley of the White River,
where the Aconcagua is born,
I came to drink, I leapt to drink
in the whip of a waterfall
that fell long-maned and hard,
breaking stiff and white.
I pressed my mouth to the bubbling spring
and the holy water burned me,
and for three days my mouth bled
from that sip of the Aconcagua.

In the land of Mitla, on a day
of cicadas, of sun, and of walking,
I bent down at a well. An Indian
came to hold me over the water:
my head, like a fruit,
cupped between his palms.
I was drinking what he drank,
his face together with my face,
and in a lightning-flash I learned
that my caste was flesh of Mitla.

On the island of Puerto Rico,
heaped with blue at siesta-time,
my body still, the waves wild,
the palms like a hundred mothers,
a girl, with a graceful gesture,
broke a coconut close to my mouth,
and, like a daughter, I drank
mother-water, palm-water.
And I have never drunk more sweetness
with my body or with my soul.

A la casa de mis niñeces
mi madre me llevaba el agua.
Entre un sorbo y el otro sorbo
la veía sobre la jarra.
La cabeza más se subía
y la jarra más se abajaba.
Todavía yo tengo el valle,
tengo mi sed y su mirada.
Será esto la eternidad
que aún estamos como estábamos.

Recuerdo gestos de criaturas
y son gestos de darme el agua.

In the house of my childhood games,
my mother would bring me water.
Between one sip and the next sip
I could see her above the jar.
Her head was steadily raised
as the jar was further lowered.
I still possess that valley,
my thirst, and her gaze.
Eternity will be just this:
that we are still the way we were then.

I recall gestures of young children,
and they are gestures of giving me water.

Figure 13. The Elqui River between Montegrande and Vicuña

TODAS ÍBAMOS A SER REINAS

Todas íbamos a ser reinas,
de cuatro reinos sobre el mar:
Rosalía con Efigenia
y Lucila con Soledad.

En el Valle de Elqui, ceñido
de cien montañas o de más,
que como ofrendas o tributos
arden en rojo o azafrán,

lo decíamos embriagadas,
y lo tuvimos por verdad,
que seríamos todas reinas
y llegaríamos al mar.

Con las trenzas de los siete años,
y batas claras de percal,
persiguiendo tordos huidos
en la sombra del higueral,

de los cuatro reinos, decíamos,
indudables como el Korán,
que por grandes y por cabales
alcanzarían hasta el mar.

Cuatro esposos desposarían,
por el tiempo de desposar,
y eran reyes y cantadores
como David, rey de Judá.

Y de ser grandes nuestros reinos,
ellos tendrían, sin faltar,
mares verdes, mares de algas,
y el ave loca del faisán.

Y de tener todos los frutos,
árbol de leche, árbol del pan,

WE WERE ALL GOING TO BE QUEENS

We were all going to be queens
of four kingdoms upon the sea:
Rosalía with Efigenia
and Lucila with Soledad.

In the Elqui Valley, encircled
by a hundred mountains or more,
which, like tributes or offerings,
blaze in scarlet and saffron,

we said it, intoxicated,
and believed it to be true,
that we would all be queens
and would one day reach the sea.

With our seven-year-olds' pigtails
and our light calico smocks,
chasing fleeting thrushes
through the shadows of the fig trees,

of our four kingdoms, we said,
with Koranic certitude,
they would be so vast and great
that they would reach the sea.

Four husbands would wed us,
when it was time to wed,
and they were kings and singers
like David, king of Judah.

As our kingdoms were so great
they would have, without fail,
green seas, seas of algae,
and wild birds from Phasian land.

And since we had all the fruits,
milk trees, bread trees,

el guayacán no cortaríamos
ni morderíamos metal.

Todas íbamos a ser reinas,
y de verídico reinar;
pero ninguna ha sido reina
ni en Arauco ni en Copán.

Rosalía besó marino
ya desposado con el mar,
y al besador, en las Guaitecas,
se lo comió la tempestad.

Soledad crió siete hermanos
y su sangre dejó en su pan,
y sus ojos quedaron negros
de no haber visto nunca el mar.

En las viñas de Montegrande,
con su puro seno candeal,
mece los hijos de otras reinas
y los suyos nunca-jamás.

Efigenia cruzó extranjero
en las rutas, y sin hablar,
le siguió, sin saberle nombre,
porque el hombre parece el mar.

Y Lucila, que hablaba a río,
a montaña y cañaveral,
en las lunas de la locura
recibió reino de verdad.

En las nubes contó diez hijos
y en los salares su reinar,
en los ríos ha visto esposos
y su manto en la tempestad.

we would not cut the lignum vitae
or bite into anything metal.

We were all going to be queens,
and we would truly reign,
but none of us has been a queen
in either Arauco or Copán.

Rosalía kissed a sailor
already wedded to the sea,
and in Guaitecas he who kissed her
was gulped down by the storm.

Soledad reared seven brothers
and left her blood in her bread,
and her eyes turned black
from never having seen the sea.

In the vineyards of Montegrande,
on her pure white breast,
she rocks the sons of other queens
and never ever her own.

Efigenia crossed paths with a stranger,
and without saying a word
she followed him, not knowing his name,
for men look like the sea.

And Lucila, who talked to rivers,
to mountains and to thickets,
truly came into her kingdom
in the moons of her madness.

In clouds, she counted ten sons;
in the salt marshes, she reigned;
in the rivers she saw her husbands,
and in storms her royal gown.

Pero en el Valle de Elqui, donde
son cien montañas o son más,
cantan las otras que vinieron
y las que vienen cantarán:

"En la tierra seremos reinas,
y de verídico reinar,
y siendo grandes nuestros reinos,
llegaremos todas al mar."

But in the Elqui Valley, amongst
a hundred mountains or more,
the others who came are singing,
and those who come will sing:

"On earth we shall be queens
and we shall truly reign,
and as our kingdoms are so vast,
we shall all reach the sea."

Figure 14. Montegrande at around the time of G.M.'s death. Her tomb is sited among the trees on the hillside to the right.

COSAS

A Max Daireaux

1

Amo las cosas que nunca tuve
con las otras que ya no tengo:

Yo toco un agua silenciosa,
parada en pastos friolentos,
que sin un viento tiritaba
en el huerto que era mi huerto.

La miro como la miraba;
me da un extraño pensamiento,
y juego, lenta, con esa agua
como con pez o con misterio.

2

Pienso en umbral donde dejé
pasos alegres que ya no llevo,
y en el umbral veo una llaga
llena de musgo y de silencio.

3

Me busco un verso que he perdido,
que a los siete años me dijeron.
Fue una mujer haciendo el pan
y yo su santa boca veo.

4

Viene un aroma roto en ráfagas;
soy muy dichosa si lo siento;
de tan delgado no es aroma,
siendo el olor de los almendros.

Me vuelve niños los sentidos;
le busco un nombre y no lo acierto,
y huelo el aire y los lugares
buscando almendros que no encuentro.

THINGS

For Max Daireaux

1

I love the things I never had
as well as those I have lost:

I touch a silent water
at rest in chilly pastures,
shimmering even with no breeze
in the orchard that was my orchard.

I look at it as I used to;
it brings me strange thoughts,
and I slowly play with this water
as with fish or with mystery.

2

I think of a threshold where I left
joyous footsteps I no longer take,
and on that threshold I see a wound
filled with moss and silence.

3

I search for a rhyme I have lost,
told to me when I was seven.
She was a woman baking bread,
and I still see her saintly lips.

4

A broken aroma arrives in gusts;
I am so happy to sense it –
so delicate it is no aroma,
being the scent of almond blossom.

It makes my senses children;
I seek its name without finding it,
and I inhale the air and places
looking in vain for the almond trees.

5

Un río suena siempre cerca.
Ha cuarenta años que lo siento.
Es canturía de mi sangre
o bien un ritmo que me dieron.

O el río Elqui de mi infancia
que me repecho y me vadeo.
Nunca lo pierdo; pecho a pecho,
como dos niños, nos tenemos.

6

Cuando sueño la Cordillera,
camino por desfiladeros,
y voy oyéndoles, sin tregua,
un silbo casi juramento.

7

Veo al remate del Pacifíco
amoratado mi archipiélago,
y de una isla me ha quedado
un olor acre de alción muerto . . .

8

Un dorso, un dorso grave y dulce,
remata el sueño que yo sueño.
Es al final de mi camino
y me descanso cuando llego.

Es tronco muerto o es mi padre
el vago dorso ceniciento.
Yo no pregunto, no lo turbo.
Me tiendo junto, callo y duermo.

9

Amo una piedra de Oaxaca
o Guatemala, a que me acerco,
roja y fija como mi cara
y cuya grieta da un aliento.

5

A river sounds always close by;
I have felt it for forty years.
It's a humming in my blood
or else a rhythm they gave me.

Or the Elqui River of my childhood,
which I breast and wade through.
I never lose it: breast to breast,
like two children, we hug each other.

6

When I dream of the mountain range
I am walking through deep gorges,
and I keep hearing, without cease,
a whistle that's almost an oath.

7

I see my archipelago
crowning the purple Pacific,
and from one of its islands I keep
the stench of dead halcyon . . .

8

A back, a solemn and gentle back
ends the dream that I dream.
It is the end of my road,
and I rest when I reach it.

Is this vague and ash-hued back
a dead tree trunk or my father?
I don't ask and don't disturb it
but lie beside it, keep quiet, sleep.

9

I love a stone from Oaxaca
or Guatemala, which I approach,
as flushed and fixed as my face
and with a breathing fissure.

Al dormirme queda desnuda;
no sé por qué yo la volteo.
Y tal vez nunca la he tenido
y es mi sepulcro lo que veo.

When I fall asleep it is naked;
I don't know why I turn it over.
Or perhaps I never held it,
and what I see is my grave.

Criaturas

MUJERES CATALANAS

"Será que llama y llama vírgenes
la vieja mar epitalámica;
será que todas somos una
a quien llamaban Nausicaa."

"Que besamos mejor en dunas
que en los umbrales de las casas,
probando boca y dando boca
en almendras dulces y amargas."

"Podadoras de los olivos,
y moledoras de almendrada,
descendemos de Montserrat
por abrazar la marejada . . ."

Creatures

CATALONIAN WOMEN

"Perhaps the ancient sea of wedding songs
to virgins calls and calls.
Perhaps we all make up the one
whom they named Nausicaa.

"So we kiss better down in the dunes
than in the doorways of our houses,
with sweet and bitter almonds
in our tasting and giving of mouth.

"Pruners of olive trees
and grinders of almond milk,*
we all come down from Montserrat
to embrace the swell of the tide . . ."

Almendrada: drink made of milk, almonds, and sugar.

115

IV

WINE PRESS
(1954)

LAGAR

Locas Mujeres

LA OTRA

Una en mí maté:
yo no la amaba.

Era la flor llameando
del cactus de montaña;
era aridez y fuego;
nunca se refrescaba.

Piedra y cielo tenía
a pies y a espaldas
y no bajaba nunca
a buscar "ojos de agua".

Donde hacía su siesta,
las hierbas se enroscaban
de aliento de su boca
y brasa de su cara.

En rápidas resinas
se endurecía su habla,
por no caer en linda
presa soltada.

Doblarse no sabía
la planta de montaña,
y al costado de ella,
yo me doblaba.

La dejé que muriese,
robándole mi entraña.
Se acabó como el águila
que no es alimentada.

Mad Women

THE OTHER

I killed a woman inside me:
a woman I did not love.

She was the flaming flower
of the mountain cactus;
she was barrenness and fire;
she never slaked her thirst.

She had stone and sky
at her feet and her back;
she never came down
in search of "water eyes".

Where she lay to rest,
the weeds shrivelled up
from her burning breath
and the flame of her face.

Her words hardened
like swift resins,
from not falling into
pure released waters.

This mountain plant
knew not how to bend,
but at her side
I was bent double.

I let her die,
robbing her of my heart.
She perished like an eagle
left alone to starve.

Sosegó el aletazo,
se dobló, lacia,
y me cayó a la mano
su pavesa acabada . . .

Por ella todavía
me gimen sus hermanas,
y las gredas de fuego
al pasar me desgarran.

Cruzando yo les digo:
"Buscad por las quebradas
y haced con las arcillas
otra águila abrasada.

Si no podéis entonces
¡ay!, olvidadla.
Yo la maté. ¡Vosotras
también matadla!"

Her wing-beat stilled,
she collapsed limply,
and her withered ashes
fell into my hands . . .

Her sisters rebuke me
still with her memory
and fiery pieces of clay
rend me as they pass.

When we meet I say to them:
"Look through the ravines
and with these clays make
another burnt eagle.

If you cannot, then,
oh!, forget her.
I killed her. Your
turn now to kill her too!"

Guerra

CAÍDA DE EUROPA

A Roger Caillois

Ven, hermano, ven esta noche
a rezar con tu hermana que no tiene
hijo ni casta presente.
Es amargo rezar oyendo el eco
que un aire vano y un muro devuelven.
Ven, hermano, o hermana, por los claros
del maizal antes que caiga el día
demente y ciego, sin saber qué pena
la que nunca penó y acribillada
de fuegos y ahogada de humareda
arde la Vieja Madre que nos tuvo
dentro de su olivar y de su viña.

Solamente la Gea americana
vive su noche con olor de trébol,
tomillo y mejorana y escuchando
el rumor de castores y de martas
y la carrera azul de la chinchilla.
Tengo vergüenza de mi *Ave* rendida
que apenas si revuela por mis hombros
o sube y cae en gaviota alcanzada,
mientras la Madre en aflicción espera,
mirando fija un cielo de azabache
que juega a rebanarle la esperanza
y grita "No eres" a la Vieja Noche.

Somos los hijos que a su Madre nombran
sin saber a estas horas si es la misma
y con el mismo nombre nos responde,
o si mechados de metal y fuego
arden sus miembros llamados Sicilia,
Flandes, la Normandía y la Campania.

War

THE FALL OF EUROPE
For Roger Caillois

Come brother, come tonight
to pray with your sister who has
no son or mother or lineage here.
It is bitter to pray hearing the echo
thrown back by empty air and a wall.
Come, brother or sister, through the rows
in the maize field before this blind,
demented day passes, not knowing
what afflicts the one who never suffered;
now, riddled with fires and choked with smoke,
our Old Mother is burning, she who bore us
amidst her olive groves and vineyards.

Only the Gaia of the Americas
lives her night with the scent of clover,
thyme, and marjoram, listening
to the sound of beavers and martens
and the blue course of chinchilla.
I am ashamed of my preferred *Ave*,
barely wheeling around my shoulders
or rising and falling like a stricken gull,
while the Mother waits in her affliction,
staring fixedly at a jet-black sky
that plays with carving up her hope
and cries "You are not" to Old Night.

We are the children who name their Mother
not knowing by now if she is still the same
and will answer us in the same name,
or if, stuffed with metal and fire,
her limbs called Sicily, Flanders,
Normandy, and Campania are in flames.

Para la compunción y la plegaria
bastan dos palmos de hierbas y de aire.
Hogaza, vino y fruta no acarreen
hasta en el día de leticia y danza
y locos brazos que columpien ramos.
En esta noche, ni mesa punteada
de falerno feliz ni de amapolas;
tampoco el sollozar; tampoco el sueño.

For compunction and pleading
a little patch of herbs and air suffice.
Bring no loaves, wine, or fruit
until the day of rejoicing and dancing
and mad arms waving branches.
For tonight: no table brightly decked
with flagons of Falerno or with poppies;
and no weeping; and no sleep.

Figure 15. Montegrande: monument to G.M. in the square

HOSPITAL

Detrás del muro encalado
que no deja pasar el soplo
y me ciega de su blancura,
arden fiebres que nunca toco,
brazos perdidos, caen manando,
ojos marinos miran, ansiosos.

En sus lechos penan los hombres,
metales blancos bajo su forro,
y cada uno dice lo mismo
que yo, en la vaina de su sollozo.

Uno se muere con su mensaje
en el desuello del fruto mondo,
y mi oído iba a escucharlo
toda la noche, rostro con rostro.

Hacia el cristal de mi desvelo,
adonde baja lo que ignoro,
caen dorsos que no sujeto,
rollos de partos que no recojo,
y vienen carnes estrujadas
de lagares que no conozco.

Juntos estamos, según las cañas,
oyéndonos como los chopos,
y más distantes que Ghea y Sirio,
y el pobre coipo del faisán rojo.

Porque yo tengo y ellos tienen
muro yerto que vuelve el torso,
y no deja acudir los brazos,
ni se abre al amor deseoso.

El Celador costado blanco
nunca se parte en grietas de olmo,

HOSPITAL

Behind the whitewashed wall,
which allows no breeze to pass
and blinds me with its whiteness,
burn fevers I never touch,
arms cut off fall oozing,
anxious blue eyes gaze out.

In its beds men suffer,
white metals under their covers,
and each of them says the same
as I, in the casing of their sobbing.

One is dying with his message
in the peeling of clean fruit,
and my ear was going to listen
to him, all night, face to face.

Down to the window-pane of my vigil,
where what I don't know descends,
fall backs I do not support,
birthing cloths I do not gather;
and squashed bodies come
from wine presses I do not know.

We are together, just like reeds,
hearing us like black poplars,
and more distant than Gaia and Sirius
and the poor beaver from the red pheasant.

Because I have and they have
a stout wall that turns our torsos
and prevents our arms from reaching out,
refusing to open to desirous love.

The white-flanked Caretaker
never splits into slivers of elm,

y aunque me cele como un hijo
no me consiente ir a los otros:
espalda lisa que me guarda
sin volteadura y sin escorzo.

El Sordo quiere que vivamos
todos perdidos, juntos y solos,
sabiéndonos y en nuestra búsqueda,
en laberinto blanco y redondo,
hoy al igual de ayer, lo mismo
que en un cuento de hombre beodo,
aunque suban, del otro canto
de la noche, cuellos ansiosos,
y me nombren la Desvariada,
el que hace señas y el Niño loco.

and though he watches me like a son,
he does not let me join the others:
a smooth back keeping watch on me
neither twisted nor foreshortened.

The Deaf One wants us all to live
lost, together, and alone,
knowing ourselves too in our quest,
in a white, circular labyrinth;
today just like yesterday, as in
a tale told by a drunkard,
though anxious necks may rise up
from the far side of night
and the sign-maker and the mad Child
call me the Delirious One.

Jugarretas

AYUDADORES
A María Fernanda de Mélida

Mientras el niño se me duerme,
sin que lo sepa ni la tierra,
por ayudarme en acabarlo
sus cabellos hace la hierba,
sus deditos la palma-dátil
y las uñas la buena cera.
Los caracoles dan su oído
y la fresa roja su lengua,
y el arroyo le trae risas
y el monte le manda paciencias.

(Cosas dejé sin acabar
y estoy confusa y con vergüenza:
apenas sienes, apenas habla,
apenas bulto que le vean.)

Los que acarrean van y vienen,
entran y salen por la puerta
trayendo orejitas de *cuye*
y unos dientes de concha-perla.

Tres Navidades y será otro,
de los tobillos a la cabeza:
será talludo, será recto
como los pinos de la cuesta.

Y yo iré entonces voceándolo
como una loca por los pueblos,
con un pregón que van a oírme
las praderías y los cerros.

Bad Moves

HELPERS
To María Fernanda de Mélida

While the baby falls asleep on me,
unbeknown even to earth,
to help me complete him
the grass makes his hair,
the date-palm his tiny fingers,
and fine beeswax his nails.
The snails give his hearing
and the red strawberry his tongue,
and the brook brings him laughter
and the hills send him patience.

(I left things unfinished
and feel confused and ashamed;
scarcely temples, hardly speech,
scarcely a shape you can see.)

The carters come and go,
in and out of the door,
bringing tiny chipmunk ears
and mother-of-pearl teeth.

Three Christmases and he will be other,
changed from head to toe:
he will stand tall and as upright
as the pine trees on the slope.

And I shall then go through the towns
like a madwoman, proclaiming him,
and my street cry will be heard
by the meadows and the hills.

131

Vagabundaje

EMIGRADA JUDÍA

Voy más lejos que el viento oeste
y el petrel de tempestad.
Paro, interrogo, camino
¡y no duermo por caminar!
Me rebanaron la Tierra
sólo me han dejado el mar.

Se quedaron en la aldea
casa, costumbre, y dios lar.
Pasan tilos, carrizales
y el Rhin que me enseñó a hablar.
No llevo al pecho las mentas
cuyo olor me haga llorar.
Tan sólo llevo mi aliento
y mi sangre y mi ansiedad.

Una soy a mis espaldas
otra volteada al mar:
mi nuca hierve de adioses,
y mi pecho de ansiedad.

Ya el torrente de mi aldea
no da mi nombre al rodar
y en tierra y aire me borro
como huella en arenal.

A cada trecho de ruta
voy perdiendo mi caudal:
una oleada de resinas,
una torre, un robledal.
Suelta mi mano sus gestos
de hacer la sidra y el pan
¡y aventada mi memoria
llegaré desnuda al mar!

Wandering

THE JEWISH REFUGEE

I travel farther than the west wind,
farther than the stormy petrel.
I pause; I question; I walk –
I never sleep for walking.
They have carved up my Earth
and have left me only the sea.

My household god, habits, and home
have stayed behind in my village.
Lime trees and reedbeds pass by,
and the Rhine that taught me to speak.
My breast bears no mint leaves,
whose scent might make me weep.
I have brought only my breath,
and my blood, and my fear.

I am one woman if I look back,
another with my face to the sea:
my nape seethes with farewells
and my breast with fear.

Now the brook in our village
flows on without saying my name:
like a footprint in the sand,
I am erased from air and land.

With each stretch of the road
I lose part of my wealth:
the scent of pine resin,
a tower, a grove of oaks.
My hand abandons its skill
at making cider and bread.
When my memory is blown away
I will come naked to the sea.

Tiempo

AMANECER

Hincho mi corazón para que entre
como cascada ardiente el Universo.
El nuevo día llega y su llegada
me deja sin aliento.
Canto como la gruta que es colmada
canto mi día nuevo.

Por la gracia perdida y recobrada
humilde soy sin dar y recibiendo
hasta que la Gorgona de la noche
va, derrotada, huyendo.

MAÑANA

Es ella devuelta, es ella devuelta.
Cada mañana la misma y otra.
Que lo esperado ayer y siempre
ha de llegar esta mañana:

Mañanas de manos vacías,
que prometieron y defraudaron.
Mirar abrirse otra mañana
saltar como el ciervo del Este
despierta, feliz y nueva,
vívida, alácrita y rica de obras.

Alce el hermano la cabeza
caída al pecho y recíbala.
Sea digno de que la salta
y como alción se lanza y sube
alción dorado que baja cantando
¡Aleluya, aleluya, aleluya!

Time

DAYBREAK

I make my heart swell to welcome
the burning cascade of the Universe.
New day comes and its arrival
leaves me breathless.
I sing like an overflowing cave,
I sing to my new day.

Grace lost and regained
makes me humble, receiving without
giving, till the Gorgon of night
runs vanquished in flight.

MORNING

She's back again, she's back again!
Every morning the same yet other.
What's hoped for yesterday and ever
must arrive this morning:

Mornings of empty hands
that promised and disappointed.
Watching another morning open,
leaping like the eastern stag,
awakened, happy and new,
vivid, diligent, and rich in works.

Brother, raise your sunken head
from your chest and let it in.
Be worthy to leap into it and be
like a halcyon,* plunging and soaring,
the gilded halcyon descending singing
'Alleluia, alleluia, alleluia!'

---

* Mythical seabird that lays its eggs on beaches in the calm mid-winter: hence 'halcyon-days'.

ATARDECER

Siento mi corazón en la dulzura
fundirse como ceras:
son un óleo tardo
y no un vino mis venas,
y siento que mi vida se va huyendo
callada y dulce como la gacela.

NOCHE

Las montañas se deshacen,
el ganado se ha perdido;
el sol regresa a su fragua:
todo el mundo se va huido.

Se va borrando la huerta,
la granja se ha sumergido
y mi cordillera sume
su cumbre y su grito vivo.

Las criaturas resbalan
de soslayo hacia el olvido,
y también los dos rodamos
hacia la noche, mi niño.

DUSK

I feel my heart melting
like candles in its sweetness:
my veins a sluggish oil
and not a wine,
and I feel my life fleeing
silent and gentle as a gazelle.

NIGHT

The mountains dissolve;
the sheep have strayed;
the sun returns to its forge:
everyone is fleeing away.

The orchard is fading;
the farm is submerged,
and my mountain range hushes
its summit and lively call.

Creatures are slipping
sideways to oblivion,
and the two of us also, dear child,
are wandering into night.

Epílogo

ÚLTIMO ÁRBOL
A Óscar Castro

Esta solitaria greca
que me dieron en naciendo:
lo que va de mi costado
a mi costado de fuego;

Lo que corre de mi frente
a mis pies calenturientos;
esta Isla de mi sangre,
esta parvedad de reino,

yo lo devuelvo cumplido
y en brazada se lo entrego
al último de mis árboles,
a tamarindo o a cedro.

Por si en la segunda vida
no me dan lo que ya dieron
y me hace falta este cuajo
de frescor y de silencio.

Y yo paso por el mundo
en sueño, carrera o vuelo,
en vez de umbrales de casas,
quiero árbol de paradero.

Le dejaré lo que tuve
de ceniza y firmamento,
mi flanco lleno de hablas
y mi flanco de silencio;

Soledades que me di,
soledades que me dieron,
y el diezmo que pagué al rayo
de mi Dios dulce y tremendo;

Epilogue

THE LAST TREE
To Oscar Castro

This solitary fretwork
they gave me at birth:
which runs from my flank
to my flank of fire;

which runs from my forehead
to my feverish feet;
this Island of my blood,
this paucity of kingdom,

I give back fulfilled
and donate in armfuls
to the last of my trees,
to tamarind or cedar.

In case in the second life
they withhold what they gave,
and I miss this oasis
of freshness and silence,

and I pass through the world
in dream, race, or flight,
wanting not house thresholds
but a tree to come home to.

I shall leave what I had
of ash and firmament,
my flank full of speech
and my flank full of silence;

the loneliness I gave myself,
the loneliness they gave me,
and the tithe I paid the lightning
of my gentle, severe God;

mi juego de toma y daca
con las nubes y los vientos,
y lo que supe, temblando,
de manantiales secretos.

¡Ay, arrimo tembloroso
de mi Arcángel verdadero,
adelantado en las rutas
con el ramo y el ungüento!

Tal vez ya nació y me falta
gracia de reconocerlo,
o sea el árbol sin nombre
que cargué como a hijo ciego.

A veces cae a mis hombros
una humedad o un oreo
y veo en contorno mío
el cíngulo de su ruedo.

Pero tal vez su follaje
ya va arropando mi sueño
y estoy, de muerta, cantando
debajo de él, sin saberlo.

my game of give and take
with the clouds and the winds
and what I learned, trembling,
from secret springs of water.

Oh, the tremulous support
of my true Archangel,
going before me down paths
with branch and balm!

Perhaps it was already born,
and I lack the grace to own it;
maybe it was the nameless tree
I carried like a blind son.

At times on my shoulders
falls moisture or breeze,
and all around me I see
the girdle of its fringe.

But perhaps its foliage
is already cladding my dream,
and, in death, I am singing
beneath it, unknowing.

Figure 16. G.M.'s funeral procession in Vicuña

V

POEM OF CHILE
(1967)

POEMA DE CHILE

Padre-Desierto

DESPERTAR

Dormimos. Soñé la Tierra
del Sur, soñé el Valle entero,
el pastal, la viña crespa,
y la gloria de los huertos.
¿Qué soñaste tú, mi niño
con cara tan placentera?

Vamos a buscar chañares
hasta que los encontremos,
y los guillaves prendidos
a unos quiscos del infierno.
El que más coge convida
a otros dos que no cogieron.
Yo no me espino las manos
de niebla que me nacieron.
Hambre no tengo, ni sed
y sin virtud doy o cedo.
¿A qué agradecerme así
fruto que tomo y entrego?

Father-Desert

WAKING UP

We slept; I dreamt of the Land
of the South, dreamt of the whole Valley:*
the pasture, the curled vineyards,
the splendour of the orchards.
What did you dream, my child,
to bring such pleasure to your face?

We'll go and look for chañar trees,†
search until we find them
and the dragon fruit growing
on the cactus from hell.‡
The one who picks most will share
with the two who picked none.
No thorns can prick my hands
as they were born from fog.
I feel no hunger or thirst;
without virtue I offer or give.
So why thank me for fruit
that I pick and hand over?

* The Elqui Valley of her childhood. See following poem.

† Chañar is a Chilean tree growing to seven metres tall. Its fruit is sweet and edible; fermented, it makes a sort of brandy called *aloja de chañar*. Its wood is hard and used for axe and other tool handles.

‡ The species she names is the Pitahaya, *Acanthocereus pentagonus/tetragonus* (syn. Christmas cactus, crab cactus, barrel cactus), which is native to Yucatán and south-west USA. For more details visit www.obsess.com/fruit/pitahaya.

145

Valle de Elqui

MONTAÑAS MÍAS

En montañas me crié
con tres docenas alzadas.
Parece que nunca, nunca,
aunque me escuche la marcha,
las perdí, ni cuando es día
ni cuando es noche estrellada,
y aunque me vea en las fuentes
la cabellera nevada,
las dejé ni me dejaron
como a hija trascordada.

Y aunque me digan el mote
de ausente y de renegada,
me las tuve y me las tengo
todavía, todavía,
y me sigue su mirada.

Elqui Valley

MY MOUNTAINS

I was raised among mountains,
with three dozen ranged around.
It seems that never, never,
wherever my steps may be heard,
have I forgotten them, neither by day
nor by starlit night,
and even now, when pools reflect
my snow-white hair,
I never left them, nor they me
like a cast-off daughter.

And though people call me
absentee and renegade,
I had them and I have them
still now, still now,
and their gaze goes with me.

Figure 17. Montegrande: schoolroom (reconstruction)

Aconcagua

MANCHA DE TRÉBOL

Un silbo del Aconcagua
me alcanza y lleva de nuevo.
Hay un alto trebolar
con tactos de terciopelo
en donde me espera, rota,
y parada como en cerco
la ronda que comenzamos
entre la tierra y el cielo.

Si voy, entro y doy la mano,
se pone a girar de nuevo;
pero aquel que la voceaba
voz ya no da, que está yerto.

Aconcagua

PATCH OF CLOVER

A whistling from Aconcagua
reaches me and carries me on.
There is a high field of clover
like velvet to the touch,
where the roundabout we started on
is waiting for me, broken,
and fenced in to a standstill
between heaven and earth.

If I go, go in and give my hand,
it begins to turn once more;
but the one who cried its wares
is now voiceless, rigid.

Nuestro Mar

VALPARAÍSO

Se pierde Valparaíso
guiñando con sus veleros
y barcos empavesados
que llaman a que embarquemos;
pero no cuentan sirenas
con estos aventureros.

Our Sea

VALPARAÍSO

Valparaíso is fading
winking with its sailing boats
and bedecked ships,
calling us to go on board;
but sirens do not reckon
with these adventurers.

Valle Central

ALAMEDAS

Las alamedas nos siguen
y nos llevan sin saberlo
por su abierta vaina verde
que canta de su aleteo
y ríe y ríe feliz
con risa que es regodeo,
con sus troncos extasiados
y sus brazos en voleo.

La lenta y desenrollada
nos lleva, de magia adentro,
como el Rafael arcángel
en un inefable arreo,
y la marcha nos festeja
a risa y cascabeleo.

¿A dónde será que llevan
para que así las crucemos
como un corredor de gracia
que muda la marcha en vuelo?

Central Valley

POPLAR GROVES

The poplar groves follow us
and lead us, unawares,
through their green open sheath,
which sings of their rustling leaves
and laughs and laughs,
happy with laughter that is delight,
with their ecstatic trunks
and their seed-scattering limbs.

Their slow unrolling
carries us, magically inward,
like the archangel Raphael,
in an ineffable drove
and the walk fetes us
with laughter and a jingle of bells.

Where can they be taking us,
to make us traverse them
like a corridor of grace
that changes our walk into flight?

Donde empiecen humedades

TALCAHUANO

De Talcahuano se viene
un tráfago de astilleros.
Las maestranzas resuellan,
comiendo y soltando hierro,
y brillan cascos vendados
a largas huinchas de acero.

Entran barcos perdularios
y parten otros enhiestos
que van a la mar lo mismo
que atún cogido y devuelto.
Y entra y sale el mar buscando
a buceos azulencos
a los que quiere ganar
y detesta al mismo tiempo,
con él arrebata y suelta
que es el amor del maulero.

Where the Damp begins

TALCAHUANO

From Talcahuano comes
a bustle of dockyards.
The shipyards wheeze,
eating and casting-off iron;
bandaged hulks shine
with long steel tapes.

Old ships sail in listing,
and others depart shipshape,
setting out to sea like
tuna caught and thrown back.
And the sea comes in and goes out,
searching in its bluish diving
for those it wants to win
and at the same time hates;
so it carries away and lets go
with its deceiving love.

Araucanía

MANZANOS

La manzana como niña
se columpia en lo escondido
y su olor, de dulce y manso,
no arrebata los sentidos.
Huele a gracia y a bondad
cual la menta y el tomillo.
De lo dulce que comienza
para en mejilla de niño,
y juran los forasteros
que ella es lo mejor que hubimos.

Nos retiene todavía
el manzanar alto y fino,
será que se da con gusto
al que lo abaja sin ruido
y no le rompe la rama
ni lo agita y ataranta,
porque defiende los nidos.

—¿Sabes tú? Los extranjeros
nos disputan lo que hubimos
pero cubren de alabanzas
la manzana que les dimos.
Plántalas en cuanto crezcas,
no estarás arrepentido.

—Mamá, repite otra vez
aquello, aquello que has dicho,
que vamos a tener todas
sí, sí, huerta, o huertecillo.
Pero tanto tiempo dicen
eso mismo y no ha venido.

—Cree ahora a quien lo dice,
la huerta viene en camino.

Araucania

APPLE TREES

Apples, like young girls,
rock in secret places,
and their scent, sweet and gentle,
captivates our senses.
They smell of grace and goodness,
as mint does, and thyme.
Their initial sweetness
stays on a child's cheek,
and outsiders swear
they're the best thing we had.

A fine tall apple orchard
still gives us pause:
it yields its fruit willingly
to those who pick gently,
without breaking its branches
or roughly shaking them,
as they protect birds' nests.

"Do you know what? Outsiders
rob us of all that was ours
but have nothing but praise
for the apples we gave them.
Plant them as soon as you grow:
you will never regret it."

"Mama, tell me once more
that thing, that thing you said,
that we are all going to have—
yes, yes—an orchard, big or small.
But they've been saying the same
for so long, and nothing happens."

"Believe it now when they tell you:
the orchard is on its way".

157

—¿Camino?

—Sí, ya se acerca.
Está llegando, mi niño.

Figure 18. Montegrande: G.M.'s tomb

"Its way?"

"Yes, it's coming close.
It's reaching us, my child."

Figure 19. Montegrande: bust of G.M. at her tomb

Selva Austral

HELECHOS

Dónde la humedad se guarda
asistidora y mansueta
y el resuello del calor
no alcanza a la Madre Gea,
suben, suben silenciosos
como unas palabras lentas,
en silencio suben, suben
estos duendes manos quietas.

Y cuando tienen la alzada
de la garza o el flamenco,
ya descansan y se quedan
latiendo de su misterio.
¡No pasar por ellos, digo,
dejarlos, que están durmiendo!
Porque sólo yo, fantasma,
ni los doblo ni los hiero.

Óiganlos dormir, dormir
sin moverles un cabello.
Ellos no viven ni mueren,
sólo escuchan el silencio,
y con el silencio hacen
cosa que no conocemos:
sueño de niños o danzas
de unos enanos traviesos.
Quedan así entredormidos
custodiando su secreto
y tal vez mi propio sueño.

Duerman los helechos altos
callados como un secreto,
sigan latiendo dormidos
así, callando y latiendo.

Southern Forest

FERNS

Where moisture lingers,
caring and mild,
and the sun's hot breath
never reaches Mother Earth,
they reach up, reach up, silent
like long slow words,
in silence they reach up, reach up,
these unthreatening sprites.

And when they've grown as tall
as a heron or flamingo,
then they rest and stay,
waving in their mystery.
Don't walk through them, I tell you:
leave them, let them sleep!
I alone, as a ghost,
neither bend them nor break them.

Listen to them sleeping, sleeping,
without moving a hair.
They neither live nor die
but just listen to the silence
and from the silence fashion
something we cannot grasp—
children's dreams or dances
of mischievous elves.
So, they stand there dozing,
watching over their secret—
and perhaps my own dream.

The tall ferns sleep
silent as a secret:
go on waving in your sleep
like that, keeping silence and waving.

¡Qué dulce su frente fría
y su aspiración de cielo!
En el aire van y van
y restan, restan, quedados,
y se parecen al monje
que entrega en su rezo el alma.
Duerman los helechos altos
que yo guardaré su sueño.

How sweet their cold forehead
and their reaching for heaven!
In the breeze they sway and sway,
then stop, stop quite still,
just like monks
offering their soul in prayer.
Let the tall ferns sleep
while I watch over their dream.

Patagonia, la lejana

ISLAS AUSTRALES

En donde Chile cansado
por fin de rutas y espacio
quiere morir como todos,
gacela, coyote o ganso.
Él empecinado aún
ojea acalenturado
la nidada de las islas
fuera de ley y de hallazgo;
pero se acabó su reino,
su voluntad y su mando,
y se queda en Puerto Montt,
como amante defraudado,
vencido el ojo de polvo,
una vez por fin exhausto.

¿Qué va a hacer el peregrino,
el trotamundos mirando
la danza de las cien islas
que ríen o están cantando?
Viene una aguda fragancia,
una incitación, de coro báquico de niñas
tiradas a la mar libre,
vírgenes pero embriagadas.
Yo no les sigo el canto,
maña, locura ni danza.
Todas ellas son hermanas,
pero por la niebla vaga
unas parecen figuras;
todas están bautizadas
y, como las Gracias, todas
son donosas y alocadas.

Patagonia, the distant

SOUTHERN ISLANDS

Where Chile, finally tired
of travels and space,
tries to die, like all beings—
gazelle, coyote, or goose—
he still, stubborn as ever,
excitedly eyes
the network of islands
beyond law and discovery;
but his kingdom, his will,
and his command are finished,
and he stays in Puerto Montt,*
like a thwarted lover,
his eyes overcome with dust,
exhausted, once and for all.

What can the traveller do,
the globetrotter faced with
the dance of the hundred islands
laughing at, singing to him?
A sharp fragrance is wafted,
tempting, from a Bacchic chorus of girls
tossed on the open sea,
inebriated even if virgins.
I do not follow their chant,
stratagem, folly, or dance.
They are all sisters,
but in the floating mist
some are just vague shapes;
they have all been baptized
and, like the Graces, are all
as poised as they are wild.

* The "he" is the Spanish *conquistador* – either in general or meaning Pedro de Valdivia
(1497-1554), who founded Santiago and Concepción but died an atrocious death at the
hands of the Mapuche. Spanish colonial rule never reached beyond Puerto Montt, the lands
to the south being acquired through conquest by the Republic in the nineteenth century.

BIBLIOGRAPHY

Alegría, C., *Gabriela Mistral íntima*. Editorial Universo, Lima, 1968.

Alegría, F., *Genio y figura de Gabriela Mistral*. Eudeba, Buenos Aires, 1966.

Alone (Hernán Díaz Arrieta), *Gabriela Mistral*. Editorial Nascimento, Santiago de Chile, 1946.

Alone (Hernán Díaz Arrieta), *Los cuatro grandes de la literatura chilena*. Editorial Zig-Zag, Santiago de Chile, 1962.

Arce de Vázquez, M., *Gabriela Mistral, persona y poesía*. Ediciones Asonante, San Juan de Puerto Rico, 1958.

Arce de Vázquez, M., *Gabriela Mistral, the Poet and her Work*, translated by Helene Masslo Anderson. New York University Press, New York, 1964.

Arciniegas, G., "El poema inédito de Gabriela" in *Cuadernos del Congreso por la Libertad de la Cultura*, No 23, pags. 17–18. Paris, 1957.

Arias, A., *Cartas de Gabriela Mistral*. Letras del Ecuador, No. 109, Quito, 1957.

Arizmendi, J., *Gabriela Mistral, poetisa de América, opina en Argentina sobre Chile, Lugones y Pablo Neruda*. Ercilla, Santiago de Chile, 1938.

Bahamonde, M., *Gabriela Mistral en Antofagasta: años de forja y valentía*. Editorial Nascimento, Santiago de Chile, 1980.

Baker Hernández, M. F., *Gabriela Mistral and the Standards of American Criticism*. University of New Mexico, New Mexico, 1963.

Bussche, G. von dem, *Visión de una poesía*. Ediciones de la Universidad de Chile, Santiago de Chile, 1957.

Cáceres, E. de, "Alma y poesía de Gabriela Mistral" in *Poesías completas de Gabriela Mistral*. Aguilar, Madrid, 1968.

Caimano, S. R. A., *Mysticism in Gabriela Mistral*, (thesis) New York, 1967. Pageant Press International Corporation, New York, 1969.

Carrión, B., *Santa Gabriela Mistral*. Casa de la Cultura Ecuatoriana, Quito, 1956.

Concha, J., *Gabriela Mistral*. Júcar, Madrid, 1986.

Conde, C., *La obra poética de Gabriela Mistral*. EPESA, Madrid, 1970.

Dana, D., *Selected Poems* (translation). Johns Hopkins University Press, Baltimore, 1971.

Dana, D., *Index to Gabriela Mistral Papers*. Organization of American States, Washington, DC, 1982.

Escudero, A. M., *La prosa de Gabriela Mistral: Fichas de contribución a su inventario*. Ediciones de los Anales de la Universidad de Chile. Santiago de Chile, 1957.

Fernández Larraín, S., *Cartas de Amor de Gabriela Mistral*. Editorial Andrés Bello, Santiago de Chile, 1978.

Figueira, G., *De la vida y la obra de Gabriela Mistral*. Talleres Gráficos, Gaceta Comercial, Montevideo, 1959.

Figueroa, V., *La divina Gabriela*. Imprenta El Esfuerzo, Santiago de Chile, 1933.

Figueroa, V., *Gabriela Mistral, Premio Nobel*. Talleres de Blass. S. A., Madrid, 1946.

Fiol-Matta, L., "The Schoolteacher of America: Gender, Sexuality and Nation in Gabriela Mistral" in *¿Entiendes? Queer Readings, Hispanic Writings*, edited by Emilie Bergman and Paul Julian Smith. Duke University Press, Durham, North Carolina, 1995.

Gazarian-Gautier, M-L., *Gabriela Mistral: the Teacher from the Valley of Elqui*. Franciscan World Herald Press, Chicago, 1975.

Guillén de Nicolau, P., *Gabriela Mistral. Lecturas para mujeres*, 3a. ed. por Gabriela Mistral, pags. vii–xii. Editorial Porrúa, Mexico City, 1971.

Horan, E., *Gabriela Mistral: an Artist and Her People*. Organization of American States, Washington, DC, 1994.

Hughes, L., *Selected Poems* (translation). Indiana University Press, Bloomington, 1958.

Iglesias, A., *Gabriela Mistral y el modernismo en Chile*. Editorial Universitaria, Santiago de Chile, 1950.

Ladrón de Guevara, M., *Gabriela Mistral: rebelde magnífica*. Araucaria, Santiago de Chile, 1957; also, Editorial Losada, Buenos Aires, 1962.

Latcham, R. A., *Los recados de Gabriela Mistral*. El Nacional, Caracas, 7 November 1957.

Loynaz, D. M., *Gabriela y Lucila. Ensayos Literarios*. Universidad de Salamanca, Salamanca, 1993.

Mistral, G., *Poesías Completas*. Editorial Andrés Bello, Santiago de Chile, 2001.

Mistral, G., *Poesías Completas*, edited by Margaret Bates. Aguilar, Madrid, 1958.

Pinilla, N., *Biografía crítica sobre Gabriela Mistral*. Edición de la Universidad de Chile, Santiago de Chile, 1940.

Pinilla, N., *Biografía de Gabriela Mistral*. Editorial Tegualda, Santiago de Chile, 1946.

Rodig, L., "Presencia de Gabriela Mistral" in *Homenaje a Gabriela Mistral*. Anales de la Universidad de Chile, pags. 282–92, Santiago de Chile, 1957.

Rodríguez Luis, J., *Cartas de Gabriela Mistral a Juan Ramón Jiménez*. Ediciones de la Torre, Mexico City, 1951.

Rosenbaum, S. C., "Gabriela Mistral" in *Modern Women Poets of Spanish America*. Hispanic Institute in the United States, pags. 171–203, New York, 1945.

Samatan, M. E., *Gabriela Mistral, campesina del valle de Elqui*. Instituto de Amigos del Libro Argentino, Buenos Aires, 1969.

Samatan, M. E., *Los días y los años de Gabriela Mistral.* Cajica, Puebla (Mexico), 1973.

Santelices, I., *Mi encuentro con Gabriela Mistral.* Editorial del Pacífico, Santiago de Chile, 1972.

Scarpa, R. E., *Una mujer nada de tonta.* Fondo Andrés Bello, Santiago de Chile, 1976.

Scarpa, R. E., *La desterrada de su patria* (2 vols.). Editorial Nascimento, Santiago de Chile, 1977.

Silva, L., *Vida y obra de Gabriela Mistral.* Editorial Andina, Santiago de Chile, 1967.

Silva Castro, R., *Retratos literarios.* Ercilla, Santiago de Chile, 1932.

Silva Castro, R., *Producción de Gabriela Mistral de 1912 a 1918.* Ediciones de los Anales de la Universidad de Chile, pags. 7–13, Santiago de Chile, 1957.

Taylor, M. C., *Gabriela Mistral's Religious Sensibility.* University of California Press, Los Angeles, 1968.

Taylor, M. C., *Sensibilidad religiosa de Gabriela Mistral,* translated by Pilar García Noreña. Gredos, Madrid, 1975.

Teitelboim, V., *Gabriela Mistral pública y secreta.* BAT, Santiago de Chile, 1992.

Torres Rioseco, A., *Gabriela Mistral.* Editorial Castalia, Valencia, 1962.

Valery, P., Prologue. *Poèmes choisis de Gabriela Mistral.* Editions Stock, Paris, 1946.

Vitier, C., *La voz de Gabriela Mistral.* Universidad Central de las Villas, Santa Clara (Cuba), 1957.

www.ingramcontent.com/pod-product-compliance
Lightning Source LLC
Chambersburg PA
CBHW071119100726
47908CB00008B/2420